Praise for *Dirty Littl*

"Very few people can write about teen girls' sexual promiscuity with the candor, empathy, and intelligence Kerry Cohen does. She did it first with *Loose Girl*, when she looked back on her own experiences. Now, in *Dirty Little Secrets*, she expands her focus to challenge all of us to get beyond our own discomforts and judgments and look at the powerful reasons girls so often value their self-worth based on their ability to be sexually 'seen' by others. I think any girl who reads this will recognize at least one girl she knows—and that girl may be looking back at her in the mirror."

—Rosalind Wiseman, *New York Times* bestselling author
of *Queen Bees and Wannabes* and *Boys,
Girls and Other Hazardous Materials*

"As compassionate as it is enlightening, Kerry Cohen's *Dirty Little Secrets* argues for female safety and desire, and provides a road map for authentically healthy, vital sexuality."

—Jennifer Baumgardner, author of *Look Both Ways,
F 'Em*, and *Manifesta*

"Cohen's book is a must-read, for it sheds light on the truth behind the secrets and lies teens tell themselves. It exposes that a teen's 'love of sex' may just be the opposite—a fear of rejection. Women of all ages can relate and benefit from this book—I can't recommend it enough. *Dirty Little Secrets* is urgently needed."

—Amber Smith, model and star of *Dr. Drew Pinsky's
Celebrity Rehab* and *Celebrity Sex Rehab*

"So much of what is written about teens and sex is either frantically alarmist or needlessly titillating. *Dirty Little Secrets* is different—with compassion and insight, it takes us into the misunderstood and underexplored world of teen girls and promiscuity. Once a 'loose girl' herself, Kerry Cohen has 'been there'—and it shows in her empathy, her insight, and her remarkable ability to draw out the truth. *Dirty Little Secrets* busts the myths, breaks down walls, and takes us where we need to go to understand the private lives of so many young women today."

—Hugo Schwyzer, PhD, Pasadena City College, coauthor,
Beauty, Disrupted: The Carré Otis Story

"Kerry Cohen has written a book that cuts through the cacophony of noise about sex, desire, and gender, and gets to the core of what's going on for so many young women today. With an empathic eye, she looks deep into the emotional lives of girls, respecting their struggles and desires, and pointing the way forward towards a more embodied and authentic sexuality for all of us."

—Courtney E. Martin, author of *Perfect Girls, Starving Daughters* and editor at Feministing.com

Praise for Kerry Cohen's *Loose Girl*

"Cohen's brutal honesty about her relentless quest for companionship is refreshingly relatable."

—*Entertainment Weekly*

"Cohen recounts her harrowing litany of hookups through clear, poignant, spare-no-details prose."

—*Marie Claire*

"Sensual yet sophisticated…explores why people yearn to be loved."

—*Self*

"A fascinating cautionary tale…*Loose Girl* will make you contemplate your own relationships."

—*Zink*

"Her candor may help under-twenty-one readers steer clear of the whole mess, while those who survived similar ordeals will appreciate her tale of survival."

—*Booklist*

"An important look at the dynamics of female sexual power and promiscuity."

—*Kirkus*

"Cohen's memoir is a deeply poignant, desperately sad account… commendably honest and frequently excruciating to read."

—*Publishers Weekly*

"Kerry Cohen's powerful, transfixing story will be familiar to many women, most of whom won't want to admit it. In this heartfelt and authentic memoir, Cohen transcends the pain and shame of a promiscuous past, and leaves readers with a sense of triumph and hope."

—Janice Erlbaum, author of *Girlbomb:*
A Halfway Homeless Memoir

"Cohen's clear-eyed, evocative, and engaging voice draws you into this harrowing story, into the heart of her addiction. Her honesty is brave, her clarity is remarkable, her candor is disarming. No matter who you are, you will find yourself, at key moments, identifying with Cohen. And in the end, you will cheer for her hard-won happiness."

—Alison Smith, author of *Name All the Animals*

"An illuminating memoir of her misspent younger years when a desperate search for love led to a series of promiscuous sexual relationships."

—*Seattle Post Intelligencer*

"Compelling...Cohen is a fine writer. She is introspective, and there's a wry humor that penetrates *Loose Girl*."

—*Portland Oregonian*

"As soon as I got a copy of Kerry Cohen's *Loose Girl*, I knew it would be one I'd want to read."

—Rachel Kramer Bussel, *Huffington Post*

DIRTY *Little* SECRETS

DIRTY *Little* SECRETS

Breaking the Silence on Teenage Girls and Promiscuity

KERRY COHEN
AUTHOR OF *LOOSE GIRL*

sourcebooks

Published by Sourcebooks, Inc.
P.O. Box 4410, Naperville, Illinois 60567-4410
(630) 961-3900
Fax: (630) 961-2168
www.sourcebooks.com

Library of Congress Cataloging-in-Publication Data

Cohen, Kerry.
    Dirty little secrets : breaking the silence on teenage girls and promiscuity / by Kerry Cohen.
    p. cm.
    Includes bibliographical references.
    1. Teenage girls—Sexual behavior. 2. Promiscuity. I. Title.
HQ27.5.C64 2011
306.70835—dc22
                        2011007322

Printed and bound in the United States of America.
VP 10 9 8 7 6 5 4 3 2 1

To the young women who generously shared their stories,
and to those whose stories still ache to be told

CONTENTS

ACKNOWLEDGMENTS

Thanks to my tireless and supportive agent Ethan Ellenberg, to Sara Appino for seeing the potential for this book, and to my editor Shana Drehs for enthusiastically believing in the book, even when I struggled to. I'm still amazed, Shana, that you got me to the end. Thanks also to Deirdre Burgess, Regan Fisher, and Katherine Faydash for their thoughtful contributions and edits. Tremendous gratitude to April Sirianni and Heather Moore for their impressive work getting the book heard.

My writing group—Michael Guerra, Ken Olsen, Gigi Rosenberg, Katherine Schneider, Jeffrey Selin, and Ellen Urbani—helped me formulate the project and clarify the direction. My family has always been supportive—especially Michael and my two beautiful sons who accommodated my disappearance to work. Thanks to James Bernard Frost, who whisked me away to get writing done, even when we didn't.

For research help, thank you to Tiffany Kalahui and Helen Delutz.

Finally, but most of all, endless thanks to the thousands of women—young and old—and men who have sent me their stories over the years, and especially those who shared their stories for this project. Had it not been for them, for their honesty and conviction, this book couldn't exist.

Whatever is unnamed, undepicted in images, whatever is omitted from biography, censored in collections of letters, whatever is misnamed as something else, made difficult-to-come-by, whatever is buried in the memory by the collapse of meaning under an inadequate or lying language—this will become, not merely unspoken, but unspeakable.

—Adrienne Rich

LETTER TO MY TEENAGE SELF

see you. It's summer, that salty, hazy time when the sun's heat on your skin feels like the promise of something. When light breezes feel like soft kisses on your face. You're tan, sun kissed, highlighted. You're pretty, but you don't think you're pretty enough, not enough to make you worth loving.

A boy thinks you're pretty, too. You know that. I see you, the way you throw him glances, shy smiles, the way he looks back, eager. I see you, the stirring inside, the way you perk up. You're thinking, *Maybe this one will save me.* Your father is unaware. Your mother is one thousand miles away. So you go with the boy, because he's there with you. You go off into the long beach grass, behind storage sheds, into the bedroom of the rented beach house when your dad is gone. Your hands are always on him, and when they're not, your mind remains on him. Every kiss, every touch, makes you want more, more, more, and soon nothing is enough, nothing feels good enough, nothing fills you. Just like always. And you start to push for more. You start to push even though you know you shouldn't, even though you know you'll push too hard. You always do. And sure enough, the moment comes. You say, "Stay with me. Want only me. Make me better, worth something." And so you've sent him away.

I see you two nights later, as well, all the color gone from your face. You watch him, want him to look, but he never does. His friend, though—his friend looks. He smiles, leans in, and whispers in the first boy's ear. For the first time, the boy you still want glances at you and looks away. Your stomach is in knots. It's all you want, for him to come to you. So when his friend does instead, you think, *This is close enough.*

You look back, twice, three times, at the boy you like as you go, but he still doesn't turn to see. This new boy, the friend, doesn't see you looking away, or he doesn't care. He pulls you by the hand. You can't remember his name, but you know it's too late to ask. He ducks into a laundry room. I see you, your blank expression, the way you acquiesce, the way you let him take off your underwear, do what he wants, the way you turn your head, waiting for it to be over. Your father is somewhere. Your mother is nowhere. I can almost hear your thoughts: *It doesn't matter. It's just one more boy.*

Afterward, you walk back to the beach house. I see you. I do. I see the way you let your hair fall over your face. You walk quickly, eyes on the ground. "I'm sorry," I want to tell you. "You're loved. You're worthwhile. You don't have to be anything for anyone else." But you wouldn't hear me, because you're there and I'm all the way over here. You'll have to keep walking, keep hurting, and someday you'll reach a point where you say, "Enough of this." You'll think it's possible that you deserve better. You'll turn to head down another road, also difficult, but worth it. A road you will question often, wondering, *Is this really any better?* Many times, you will change directions again. Many times, you will think, *I'm not worth this.* But then you'll realize again that you are. It will be a long, tiresome road, but eventually you'll come to know what I know. For now, I see you. For now, I think, *If only someone else had seen you, too.*

Introduction

GIRLS LIKE US

ou see them everywhere. They walk along busy highways in low-
slung jeans and tank tops, peering into every car that passes.
They sit with their friends in diners and coffee shops, searching,
their thoughts clearly on who is looking at them. They catch the
eyes of the boys they pass. They smile and flip their hair. They post
photos of themselves in bikinis on Facebook. They are just girls.
They are your sister, your daughter, your friend, your niece. They
are not remarkable, really, in any way. They are almost every girl you
see. They believe in their hearts that they are worth nothing, that
they have little to offer. They believe boys will pull them out of their
ordinariness and finally, *finally*, transform them into someone better
than who they are.

They have sex too early and for the wrong reasons. They get
STDs, and they get pregnant too young. They are "friends with
benefits," but with no benefit to themselves. They give out blow
jobs like kisses and hope for love in return. They are ignored. They
don't get called. They get dumped again and again. They lie alone in

their beds and hate themselves for being so unlovable, for being so needy, for not being like every other girl, for not being able to just have fun. But they aren't sex addicts or even love addicts. What they crave is the attention, that moment when a boy looks at them and they can believe that they are worth something to someone. They can believe that they matter.

When these girls grow up, they find that in this way, they are still girls. They carry their pasts with boys into their futures. They remain needy, desperate, anxious for someone to prove their worth. The boys, though, become men.

For much of my life, I was that girl. When I became a therapist, I learned that there were many others like me. And when I wrote my memoir, *Loose Girl*, about my experiences, I heard from many, many more girls like me. They assumed that they were the only ones, that they alone suffered this peculiarity. How could this be? How do we get so far into our lives and into these experiences without sharing them—and our feelings—with our friends, our parents, or a caring adult? Because we feel so alone—because we carry immense shame about our behavior and, more so, our desperation. Some came from divorce, like I did. Others had lived through severe abuse. Still others had untarnished childhoods, intact families, and the feeling that they had been loved. Some had sex with only three men; others with fifty. The number of men isn't important. It is the *feelings* these young women experienced—that if they got a man's attention it would mean they were worth something in the world.

You might be this girl, too. Maybe in some ways you have experienced such feelings even if you never acted on them the way some of us did. You have met eyes with a man and thought, *Maybe he could save me.* You have done your makeup and dressed provocatively to attract men at an event. You aren't immune to the feeling that a man will make you feel something more than just love, more than just sexy—that he will make you feel valuable.

We aren't sex addicts or love addicts—at least not at first. We aren't diagnosable. We aren't yet to the point where we let these feelings utterly destroy our lives, even if, in some ways, it seems they do. They consume us. We are obsessed with getting love, with using male attention to make ourselves worthwhile in the world. Like the girls Courtney L. Martin describes in her book *Perfect Girls, Starving Daughter: The Frightening New Normalcy of Hating Your Body*, girls who don't have eating disorders per se but obsess over the idea of needing to be thinner than they are, the girls I discuss in this book are on a continuum of promiscuity.[1] Sex and love addictions are simply more extreme versions of what many—maybe even most—girls face regarding sex and love.

What happened to us? How did we get to this point, where we use male attention like a drug, again and again, as unsatisfying to us as it is? Why do we keep going back, even though our behavior often becomes self-destructive? And, finally, how do we move from that behavior, those feelings, toward real intimacy?

After *Loose Girl* arrived on bookshelves, readers were eager to share their stories, to voice their feelings, to know that they weren't alone. Many wanted answers, a formula, to get themselves to a new place, to stop harming themselves with their promiscuity. This book is my answer to their plea. It is a study of the cult of female, teenage promiscuity, and the silence that surrounds the topic; it is a sharing of numerous stories about the harm done and the movement toward real intimacy. It is also a genuine discussion about how we can make change for ourselves, our daughters, our clients, and our culture.

The bottom line is that we don't like to talk about teenage girls and sex. Sure, we see it everywhere. Teenage girls in provocative clothing flood the media. They have sex on *Gossip Girl* and *Degrassi* and *One Tree Hill.* And they definitely have sex on reality shows like *The Real World* and *16 and Pregnant.* But when we discuss adolescent girls and sex, it is only in one way: don't have sex. This is easier than anything else. We tell teenage girls to stay away from sexual behavior and to practice abstinence. Don't have sex, we say, because we don't like to imagine them having sex. If they do, then we have to think of them as sexual creatures, and that makes us squirm.

In fact, much of the promiscuity among young women, both heterosexual and homosexual, is likely to go undetected because it makes therapists uncomfortable. When I appeared on *Dr. Phil* to discuss two teen girls whose parents were unhappy they were having sex, the tagline next to the girls' names when they were on screen was "sexually active," as though that was a disorder or a crime of some sort.

But while we refuse to discuss teenage sex, it is happening. According to the Guttmacher Institute, although teenage sexual activity has declined 16 percent in the past fifteen years, almost half (46 percent) of all 15- to 19-year-olds have had sex at least once, and 27 percent of 13- to 16-year-olds are sexually active. The larger proportion of these teenagers are black (67.3 percent) and Hispanic (51.4 percent) rather than white (41.8 percent). Much of the sexual behavior occurs in populations traditionally thought to have less experience in sexual activity, though, such as teenagers from affluent homes and preadolescents.[2]

Ultimately, the statistics for STDs and teenage pregnancy aren't promising. We are experiencing a record high of teenage girls with sexual diseases. Of the 18.9 million new cases of STDs each year, 48 percent occur among 15- to 24-year-olds. One in four teenage girls aged 14–19 and one in every two black teenage girls has an STD. Each year, almost 750,000 teen pregnancies are reported for women aged 15–19, and 82 percent of those pregnancies are unplanned.[3] The MTV reality series *Teen Mom*, a spin-off of the wildly successful *16 and Pregnant*, had the channel's highest-rated premiere in more than a year—evidence, I'd say, of our fascination with teenage motherhood. What happens behind these statistics, the feelings and motivations behind promiscuous behavior, and the direct results of it, is less clear. These are the dirty little secrets that girls carry. These are the stories they have—we have—but don't tell.

There is some research that casual sex among teenagers can be more harmful than we've thought. The adolescent brain's prefrontal cortex—the part of the brain responsible for judgment—develops at an explosive rate. There are in fact only two times during development that the brain is overrun with synapses (neural connections) in this way: right before birth and right before puberty. At this critical time in preadolescence, the brain manufactures far more synapses than necessary. The synapses that are used become stronger. The ones that aren't used weaken and die. As a result, certain experiences become sealed in that teen's growth, in the strong synapses. If they handle intimacy—and sex—in ways that don't get them what they really want, again and again, they are likely to wind up with a potentially harmful approach to intimacy.[4]

What's more, the prefrontal cortex is not fully developed until the mid-twenties, and there is some evidence that bonding through sex and then breaking up again and again damages the ability to establish meaningful connection through intimacy. In other words, when teens bond and break, bond and break, before the cortex is fully developed, as most teens do, they potentially set themselves up for trouble with real intimacy later on. (This research, however, is based on findings concerning oxytocin, and many have argued that we don't know enough about oxytocin to make such claims. See the "References and Notes" section at the end of the book for more information.)[5]

At the same time, though, we know that a girl's ability to express her sexual desires is a necessary step toward developing healthy sexual intimacy, and it is essential if she is to protect herself against unwanted or unsafe sexual activities. In fact, in one study, researchers found that the fewer sexual partners a girl had, the more likely she was to not assert her beliefs and feelings during sexual activity, thereby potentially setting herself up for negative sexual experiences.[6]

Not all teenage sexual behavior derives from self-harm. Ideally, in fact, none of it would. Sexual curiosity and experimentation is a perfectly natural part of growing up. Girls have just as much sexual desire and curiosity as boys. They are curious about their genitals and others' as children. They masturbate. The hormones that race through a teenage girls' body create just as much sexual feeling as boys' hormones do.

Psychological discussions about why girls might engage in sexual activity, however, do not include any information about girls' sexual desire. Michelle Fine refers to this as "the missing discourse of desire" in her article of the same name.[7] She notes that we talk about victimization, violence, and morality, but we almost never examine the fact that girls, too, have desire. In fact, sexual desire is seen as an aberration for girls, which means that we almost always assume that girls act sexually only to fulfill their hopes for a relationship. This can certainly be the case, but it's potentially dangerous—as we make policy, as we aim to help girls, as we aim to help ourselves—not to account for the fact that they also experience sexual arousal.

We don't generally like to say these things about adolescent girls. We don't acknowledge that they have desire. We live in a culture that provides little space for any sort of female teenage sexual behavior, including what many would consider normal curiosity and exploration, because it makes us so uncomfortable.

How did this odd untruth about female desire arise? Ancient and medieval understandings of puberty emphasized vitality and social benefit, and they made little distinction between male and female desire. The rising influence of Christianity, though, established the beliefs that youthful sexuality was dangerous, immoral, and threatening to social order. With the Enlightenment, boys regained some freedom over their right to sexual expression, but girls' sexual desire remained deviant. Over the following centuries, while puberty for boys took on its association with manly desire, for girls it grew more and more removed from any notion of desire and instead focused entirely on preparation for reproduction and motherhood.[8] In conjunction with this, girls' experience with puberty was associated only with the need to protect their purity so they would be ready for their fate as mothers. Our notions today about girls and female desire are built on outdated patriarchal, religious notions.

Today, the cultural narrative is as follows: boys are horny, but girls are not, and so girls must do what they can to keep boys and their out-of-control hormones at bay. We like this narrative, outdated and unscientific as it is. It keeps us safe from the notion that girls might want to be sexual as much as boys do. *But*, you might be thinking, *what is the problem with keeping girls safe?* As I explore in this book, the problem is that when you deny a group of people an essential part of who they are, a part they have full right to, they often wind up using it in a self-destructive manner rather than as a natural part of their development. In other words, if teenagers getting STDs and becoming pregnant and acting out sexually is a cultural problem, then stigmatizing teenage sex only makes it worse—much worse.

The distinction between acting on natural sexual feelings and using male attention and sex to fill emptiness is an important one. In this book, I carry the underlying assumption that teenage girls have natural sexual feelings, just like boys, and that perhaps we need to find an outlet for girls to express themselves sexually, an outlet that the girls control themselves, not the cultural expectations about who they should be as sexual creatures. I also try to demarcate what it might look like when a girl has stepped beyond cultural boundaries and has begun using male attention and sex to try to feel worthwhile. And there *is* a difference: some girls manage to cope with our culture's lack of space for girls to have sexual feelings, but others struggle and tend to use sexual attention and behavior to harm themselves emotionally. So for the purposes of this book, I refer to self-destructive sexual behavior as promiscuity and to the girls who pursue such self-destructive attention as loose girls.

Without discussion, without creating the space for girls to talk about their sexual experiences, we are left with assumptions that are almost invariably wrong. If we are not virgins, we are called sluts. We get what we deserve and what we wanted. Or—and this emerging view is not as positive as it seems—we are empowered by our sexuality; we are waving our flags of sexual freedom. After all, in this day and age, to suggest that a girl having sex is anything other than empowered and strong is antifeminist.

Meanwhile, the media continues to propagate the double-edged sword, the messages that girls have always received. You must be sexy, but you may not have sex. You must make men want you, but you may not use that to fill your own desires. The women's studies professor Hugo Schwyzer calls this the Paris paradox, based on Paris Hilton's comment that she was "sexy but not sexual."[9] He notes that young women raised with Paris Hilton in the limelight were promised sexual freedom but wound up with more obligation than abandon. In other words, girls' requirement to be sexy greatly outweighs any attention to what might be a natural, authentic sense of their sexual identity.

This is not a book telling teenage girls not to have sex. On the flip side, it's also not a book that encourages promiscuity. It's a book about how we can all work together to find a way to let teenage girls stop harming themselves with their sexual behavior. It's a book—at its core—about girls' rights and sexual freedom.

The true experience of being a teenage girl these days is so lost inside all this noise, all the assumptions and messages coming from everyone but the girl herself, that we couldn't possibly know what emotions are behind promiscuous behavior. That's why I went straight to the source—finally—and asked to hear from the girls and women themselves.

I interviewed approximately seventy-five American volunteers who had originally emailed me after reading *Loose Girl*.[10] I do not claim by any stretch of the imagination to present scientific findings. These are qualitative stories from real girls who believed in this project and understood that by sharing their stories they could potentially help other girls out there who struggle with similar feelings and behaviors. Some are still teenagers, but others are older and either still act out or have learned to stop. These girls come from a range of socioeconomic backgrounds. Most are white, but about 15 percent are black, Asian American, Hispanic, and biracial. Some call their mothers their best friends. Some have never met their fathers. Some have happily married parents and eat dinner with their families at the same time each night. Some have been raped. Some got pregnant. Some have been treated for STDs. All of them have carried shame about their behavior at one time or another, and all of them have felt alone. Not one felt there were any guidelines out there to help them move out of this behavior. This book answers that need.

All of the girls and women I interviewed have been given pseudonyms to protect their privacy. In an ideal world, they would be able to claim their stories without needing confidentiality. But unfortunately, girls who talk about their sexual experiences often get bullied and ostracized. In my mind, this is more evidence of our need for these conversations, more evidence of how badly we need to normalize sexual desire and behavior among adolescent girls.

This book has two purposes. First, I want to simply open a discussion that aims to identify girls' sexual experiences in our culture, how they develop as sexual creatures inside a culture that largely holds the reins on what that means. I aim to help readers understand how girls head into adolescence as loose girls, how they often wind up using male attention and promiscuity as a way to feel worthwhile, and how that experience gets reinforced once it is under way. Second, I hope to provide some suggestions for helping girls find their way out of this negative experience with promiscuity and for protecting girls from using sex in this way in the first place.

With that intention, the book is split into two parts—identifying the loose girl experience and helping girls gain power over their sexual lives. At the beginning of each chapter, I include a quote from the girls and women who have contacted me about their own sexual experiences.

In chapter 1, I examine girlhood, from puberty on, from a sexual perspective. Here girls discuss how their identities are tied up with how teenage boys view them and how they think of themselves in relation to other people. This includes the notion that girls must measure up to a certain physical standard to be worthwhile, how they can assess that measure on the basis of male attention, and how impossible it is for a girl to ever feel that she is good enough as she is. Chapter 1 also examines the ways in which female adolescent development is perfectly poised for those sorts of belief. It briefly discusses the ways this belief has remained relatively constant throughout much of our history, and is, in this way, interwoven with the female identity, even as so many other strides have been made for women over time.

Then we'll delve into boys and discuss just what it is about them that makes them so beautiful, so free, and always so unattainable. Chapter 2 explores the fantasy that our culture builds about boys and how that gets tangled up with girls' beliefs about them. We'll look at how those fantasies get wound up with the idea that boys will free us from that particularly female belief that we aren't good enough as we are.

In chapter 3, we'll dive into that minefield that is teenage girls and sex. It is one of our long-standing taboos. And yet, teenage girls have sex. They have sexual desires and curiosity. They experiment. They have fantasies. Usually when we discuss teenage girls and sex, though, we do so in prescribed, limited ways. Girls are virgins, sluts, or empowered. In this chapter, I explore—with the help of the girls I interview and existing literature—how girls see themselves in relation to these archetypes. Together we find that they don't often fit these constrictions, and yet because of these archetypes, they feel voiceless, shamed, and alone.

Much of the research out there suggests that, for girls to have a healthy relationship to sex, they must have a healthy relationship with their mothers. Through interviews with girls and the current literature, chapter 4 examines the ways in which severed intimacy with mothers both does and doesn't contribute to promiscuous behavior. We'll also discuss the issue of mothers modeling attention-needing behavior from men, and how that influences girls' behavior as well.

Most people assume that a girl's relationship with her father determines her future with boys and men. In chapter 5, we will examine whether, and in what capacity, this has been true for girls. This examination includes fathers' behavior with women, their direct and/or indirect sexualizing of girls, and their ability to show appropriate attention to their daughters.

In chapter 6, we discuss other ways girls harm themselves in conjunction with promiscuity, such as alcohol, drugs, cutting, and eating disorders. How do these behaviors interact with promiscuity, and in what ways are they part and parcel of the same thing? We also look at the prevalence of depression and other mood disorders with promiscuous behavior.

Sex, rape, and losing virginity is chapter 7's focus. As we've discussed, teenage girls *do* have sexual desire and curiosity. Is it possible to build a society in which we can allow them to experiment sexually, to make their own choices regarding sex, without being tunneled into the archetypes available to them?

One of the challenges tied up with that question is rape. We tend to think of rape as a black-and-white issue—you either are or aren't the victim of rape. You either say yes or no. But the concept can become blurry when a girl acts out promiscuously because of low self-esteem or because she so often feels violated even when she consents. Rape is legally and clearly defined, of course, but the sense of violation many loose girls experience can have long-lasting emotional effects that are similar to the consequences of rape.

Another challenge is the fantasy world we apply to sex, particularly for adolescent girls. To lose her virginity, a girl must be in love. It will be the most magical, eventful night of her life. Much too often girls get drunk to lose their virginity so that they will have an excuse later, so they won't have to take on the aura of a girl who chooses sex. Through interviews with girls, I examine these various issues and how, with them, we might build new avenues for girls' sexual choices.

In chapter 8, we'll look at the brave new world of dating. It was the 1980s and 1990s when I was living out the scenes that I would later share in *Loose Girl*. Computers were just beginning to enter our culture. No one I knew used a cellular phone. And yet I managed to get myself into trouble with boys again and again. We'll examine how things are different now and what those differences mean in terms of promiscuous behavior. We'll also explore the dangers that may come up when a girl pursues male attention, and the newer, more complex venues for this danger to play out today.

In part 2, we'll look at a few ways that girls can gain power. Too often we assume that younger girls act out sexually but learn to control their impulses and ultimately find intimacy when they mature into women. The more common truth is that girls carry these struggles into adulthood. In chapter 9, we'll hear stories from women who still feel addicted to that attention from men.

In chapter 10, we'll explore various ways girls have come to new and better places with promiscuity and with their need for male attention, and how we can help them make those changes. We'll also look at those who haven't been able to change and the dangers involved in that inability to change, and we'll consider the possibility that change is only partially possible and depends on the particular situation of the person trying to make that change.

Ultimately, if we are to make true change for girls, we also need to transform our culture away from one that positions girls as sexual objects and only allows particular archetypal figures for girls engaging in sexual activity. Chapter 11 explores how girls might take the lead on that change, including through transformation of our sex education programs.

My hope is that women young and old, parents, therapists, and school administrators, will see this book as an opening, a break in the silence surrounding teenage girls and sex.

PART ONE

THE LOOSE GIRL

Chapter 1

GIRLS WILL BE GIRLS
Female Sexual Development

As years went by sex became exactly what I wished to win, because it told me that I was valuable and beautiful, and those things were so important to me.

When Faith was eleven years old, she went with her family to the community swimming pool like she had each summer. Every summer prior, she had pushed through those gates, pulled off her outerwear, and jumped right into the deep end. She prided herself on her back dives and her handstands and the fact that she could swim underwater from one end of the pool to the other without once coming up for air. But this summer, something was different. Faith felt hesitant. She walked more slowly. She was hyperaware of her body, of the small breasts that had ached and pressed beneath her chest during the fall and spring, and of the fact that her inner thighs now touched.

There were boys at the pool. Boys! They had been there every summer, of course. How had she not noticed? The boys didn't turn to look at her as she walked along the edge of the pool, which suddenly mattered in a terrible way. Was there something wrong with her? Was she ugly? Was she fat? Was she not sexy? Rather than jump right into the pool she lay on a lounge chair and considered how she appeared to the boys who might look at her. She lifted a leg so her thigh fat wouldn't spread. She left her sunglasses on even though that might make funny tan lines on her face, because she thought she looked good with them on—glamorous, like a movie star. Faith's mother, concerned, asked why she wasn't going in the water, but Faith just shrugged. She wasn't going to tell her mother the real reason—that she felt watched, desperate, both embarrassed that the boys would see her and terrified that they wouldn't.

Lana, just a little older than Faith, was always an exceptionally pretty girl. Her father, especially, took tremendous pride in her round, blue eyes and blond curls. When she was little, he liked to bring her to the fire station where he worked and show her off to his coworkers. His friends told him he better be careful when she grew up, and he laughed and rolled his eyes, but Lana could tell that he liked that they thought this. She was quite aware of all of this, actually—her father's admiration of and pride in her looks. And she was equally aware of her mother's jealousy over the way he treated Lana. From a very young age, she did what she could to be extra pretty. She smiled sweetly. She spoke politely to her father's friends, answering all their questions.

When she started puberty at ten years old, though, her father distanced himself. It was subtle, but it was clear: where once she had been her father's daughter, now she was handed off to her mother. Lana continued to do everything she could to be pretty, and—following cultural guidelines—sexy. She wore shirts that showed off her young breasts. She wore skirts that exposed lots of leg. She wore makeup and nail polish and perfume. Her mother felt she was out of control. Her father became stricter and told her she needed to focus on her schoolwork, not boys, which only made Lana feel betrayed.

So, at the young age of twelve, Lana began to pursue boys. She let them touch her however they wanted. She gave blow jobs regularly. She worked her way through the boys at school. At the same time, she grew withdrawn and depressed. She fought with her parents. She started bringing in bad grades. One day her mother said to her, "Where did my Lana go? I don't even know who you are anymore." Lana didn't know who she was anymore, either.

Before girls become women, they are whole, energized, excited. They take on the world without hesitation. They are their own directors, in charge of their lives. But then things almost always change. Mary Pipher famously described this seismic shift that comes about as girls enter puberty. She writes, "Just as planes and ships disappear mysteriously into the Bermuda Triangle, so do the selves of girls go down in droves. They crash and burn in a social and developmental Bermuda Triangle."[1] As girls enter adolescence, they also enter another culture, one in which how they appear to others becomes how they exist. "Girls stop being and start seeming," Pipher notes, quoting Simone de Beauvoir.[2]

Sally Mann, my favorite photographer, captures this transitional time in her collection *At Twelve: Portraits of Young Women*. In each photograph, girls are on the cusp of something. They are both children and too knowing. In some, it is obvious by the ways they hold themselves that they know too much. In others, you can see the light that has begun to fade. Ann Beattie writes in her introduction to the images, "Twelve-year-old girls know what brought them to the present moment, but that's as far as they've gotten."[3] In other words, they fully know themselves, even as they have begun this change, but they can't see where they are headed.

Boys and girls enter adolescence—they become "tweens"— already amid challenges. They go through their greatest physical and emotional growth since infancy. Puberty—a well-known test for most—comes earlier these days. Although the average age of puberty onset is 10.5, with most girls entering puberty between the age of 8 and 13, there is evidence that this age is dropping.[4] In 1997, a landmark study of approximately seventeen thousand girls found that 15 percent of Caucasian girls and 50 percent of black girls already started to show signs of puberty by age 8.[5] More recent research suggests an even further drop to age 7. A fifteen-year study out of Denmark published in 2009 determined that the average age of breast development for girls has dropped a full year—from 10.88 years to 9.86 years.[6]

Age of menarche, a girl's first period, does not seem to be lowering, however. In other words, many girls' secondary sex characteristics— breast development, pubic hair growth, and widening hips—are developing early, but first menstruation, which means ovulation and hence the ability to get pregnant, does not arrive with those secondary sex characteristics. (Researchers theorize that increasing amounts of obesity and estrogen in our environment (via Bisphenol A [BPA], pesticides, compounds in cigarettes, and phthalates) cause the earlier onset, but no studies have been conclusive.)[7] Caucasian girls' average age of menstruation is 12.6, which is not significantly earlier than it was in the 1970s. We do know, though, that black and Mexican American girls' median age of menarche has always been lower—12.06 for non-Hispanic Blacks and 12.25 for Mexican Americans.[8]

As I alluded to briefly in the introduction, when adolescence hits, there is also a vast overproduction of brain cells and neuronal connections. It is during the early teen years that kids prune out the connections they don't use. At the same time, their frontal lobes, which control judgment, logic, and organization, are not yet well developed. New teens have access to most emotions, but they don't yet have the skills to deal effectively with them.

For girls, these developmental changes are particularly affected by what happens in the environments surrounding them, and most particularly in the ways they are sexualized by our culture. The images that control our understanding of girls are, in fact, so pervasive, such an ordinary part of our lives, that they are almost unseen. To even say that girls are sexualized in our culture verges on not saying anything at all.

Images of womanhood, of who we are supposed to be, are fed to us from infancy—go to any store that sells toys and there is a distinct "girls' aisle" where everything is pink and tulle and satin. It doesn't matter that there are also career-themed Barbies, or other dolls and playthings meant to encourage independence. The point is simply that everywhere a girl looks, from the moment she comes out of the womb, but then especially once she reaches adolescence, the media establishes clearly that *it* owns her sense of self.

What we speak of less, though, is how that wave of objectification and those mixed messages—"be sexy but not slutty"—are so strong that girls really don't have a fighting chance. Magazines, billboards, commercials, Internet ads—these are just the tip of the iceberg. Take a quick glance at some of the top teen girls' magazines and you see these headlines: "How to Get a Guy's Attention," "383 Ways to Look Hot," "Look Pretty," "How to Get Perfect Skin," "Get Pretty Now," and "Be Irresistible." Girls see more than four hundred advertisements per day telling them how they should look.[9] The images are so pervasive that we barely notice them.

Naomi Wolf calls the sexy-but-not-slutty images "flattened beauty," attractiveness defined by a cultural ideal that has nothing to do with girls' organic, individual beauty.[10] Airbrushed bodies and flawless faces sit on the cover of every popular women's magazine. The television runs a reel of size zeros and twos, of symmetrical faces and perfectly styled hairdos. Such people populate some of the most popular shows teenagers watch—*iCarly*, *Gossip Girl*, *The Vampire Diaries*, and *Glee*. Models, celebrities, and pop stars plaster advertisements, billboards, and screens. These people are all we see, which is a constant reminder to average-looking people that we are not that, but that we should certainly spend every moment trying to be that if we, too, want to be seen.

The most pervasive and scrupulous of these images, however, are the ones pertaining to sex and romance. Everywhere we look is a carefully designed suggestion of sexiness and the clear message that girls' primary interest should be getting a boy's attention through her looks. Open any teen magazine. Watch any commercial aimed at teen girls. She washes her face, wears a tampon, buys school supplies, and wears sneakers all in some sexy manner that reveals the intention of getting boys to notice her. And it starts way earlier than the teen years—just about every Disney princess plot revolves around snagging a man. *The Little Mermaid* is a perfect example. The main character Ariel doesn't even speak, and then she gives up her entire identity as a mermaid and singer to get her guy. The meaning has been the same for decades: be available but not too available and, most important, get male attention at all costs. Girls have limited choices in how to respond to these messages. If they want social acceptance, though, the options vanish and there is really only one message left: "be sexy but not sexual." The message is only made worse by the sheer number of outlets available to deliver it.

Even those images that seem to support independence and strength—ass-kicking girls like Buffy the Vampire Slayer and Veronica Mars, or self-contained girls like Bella's character in the *Twilight* movies or Elena Gilbert on *The Vampire Diaries*—often maintain impossible standards of attractiveness. More important, they are almost always caught up in the process of trying to make a boy love them or of keeping a boy's love. Bella, for instance, is painted as an everygirl. In the *Twilight* books she is not supposed to be anywhere near as attractive as the actress who plays her in the movies. But even in her ordinariness, a stunningly gorgeous vampire wants her and only her. He has eyes for no one else. Bella begins as a self-contained teenage girl who knows who she is and is not swayed by others' opinions of her, but soon after Edward falls for her, her entire existence hinges on his love. Stephenie Meyer encourages a fantasy most all girls have: to be as plain as they are but to be adored and chosen by a really hot, really respectful guy.

Elena from *The Vampire Diaries* is exceedingly attractive, so it makes perfect sense that two hot vampire brothers spend much of their time trying to get with her. Although Elena's character, like Bella's, is supposed to be independent, not swayed by boys, the plot shifts soon enough so that her entire life depends on the love she shares with the brothers.

Yes, we've had shows like *Ugly Betty*, starring a more realistic looking female someone who didn't have that "flattened beauty," who didn't spend all the episodes trying desperately to be loved. But the show was so unique in this way that the entire plotline had to involve the fact that she wasn't our cultural ideal. The show's name even called this very attractive woman "ugly"! And anyway, while viewers raved for one season, by the second season, they were over it, ratings fell, and the show was canceled. This disappearance is familiar. Darlene Conner from *Roseanne* and Angela Chase from *My So-Called Life*, also long gone, were strong, sarcastic characters who really didn't care what you thought of them—but even then, cool, plain Angela spent pretty much all her on-screen time chasing Jared Leto's character, who was, let's face it, super good looking but equally vapid and dumb.

Recently, Lauren Zizes's character on *Glee* gives new hope. Puck, the attractive, popular player, falls for her. First, the focus is on her large shape. He tells her he loves her curvy body, but, unimpressed, she says, "I look like what America looks like." Finally he admits he likes most that she's more of a badass than he is.

Even if we were to assume that a violent female, an "ass-kicking" female, equals a strong female, one study found that in films where females participated in violent action, 58 percent of those female characters were portrayed as submissive to the male lead and 42 percent were in romantic relationships with them.[11]

So, even Lauren Zizes is guilty of this. (Her character still defies all expectations of what's come before, and, hey, she's on prime time, so I cannot feel disappointed.)

If our media has an obsession with romance and love, then it shows sexiness to girls as the way to get that romance. Generally, when we talk about girls in the media, people express outrage about excessively sexy images, which they argue lead to promiscuity. It's true that sexual behavior and images of sex in our media have increased rapidly over the decades. Partially, this is simply because of increased tolerance for sexual imagery. Also, the modes of technology—places where we can see those images—have multiplied. But I would argue that our concerns about sexualization are mostly misguided. When given a bare-backed, tousled-hair photo of Miley Cyrus, only adults see a postcoital image. Kids generally don't pick up on the subtleties of sex in images until they become more sexually experienced. Images alone don't create promiscuity. The real problem is that girls see those images as their tickets to male attention and romance.

Diane Levin and Jean Kilbourne write in their book *Sexy So Soon*: "[S]ex in commercial culture has far more to do with trivializing and objectifying sex than with promoting it, more to do with consuming than with connecting. The problem is not that sex as portrayed in the media is sinful, but that it is synthetic and cynical."[12] In other words, our media shows sex as something artificial, unnatural, maybe even porn influenced. Think about some of today's female singers, such as Ke$ha, Rihanna, and Beyoncé, who have expressed their sexuality by accentuating cleavage, wearing stripper heels, and pouting at the camera. How does that have anything to do with real sex or intimacy? Girls learn that male attention—and potentially then romance and love—comes from *appearing* artificially sexy.

And yet these singers, like most of those in the media outlets that exploit sexuality, are not trying to do anything other than appeal to our demands. Girls want direction for attracting men, and this is how to do it: girls need only learn how to appeal to boys' sexual desire. Girls take notes on how to make themselves desirable, on how to move, dress, pout, and wear makeup. For the purpose of selling things, learning how to court the male desire for real companionship or intimacy isn't nearly as provocative.

But while the media images encourage sexiness, institutions such as the National Abstinence Education Association, Focus Adolescent Services, and the National Campaign to Prevent Teen and Unplanned Pregnancy pressure girls to not be sexual at all. In fact, the institutions seem as obsessed with trying to control girls' sexuality as the media does. Parents and schools often exert this antisexual pressure as well.

In today's culture, abstinence and virginity connote morality for girls in a way that's different from that for boys. That is, although we reference honor and strength and basic moral ideals when we teach boys about being good, we mostly reference virginity for girls. As Jessica Valenti notes in *The Purity Myth*, "While boys are taught that the things that make them men—good men—are universally accepted ethical ideals, women are led to believe that our moral compass lies somewhere between our legs."[13] Virginity is not just a sexual choice; it's the most prominent way to frame who you are as a person.

Valenti also identifies the "desirable virgin," the feminine ideal of our culture, who is both sexy and not sexual (we'll explore more about the virgin myth in chapter 3).[14] As most of us know, living up to such expectations is all but impossible, but it is particularly tricky for the adolescent girl who is dealing with new sexual curiosity and developmental challenges. On the one hand is abstinence-only education and on the other hand is the push to make themselves desirable: girls learn quickly that there is no happy medium.

The images and pressures are indeed so tremendous that it is sometimes hard to remember that beneath all of it there is a girl who has genuine sexual curiosity and desire, a girl who suddenly is receiving massive amounts of attention not for her intelligence or sense of humor, but for her body.

In *Loose Girl*, I wrote about how, at the age of eleven, walking on the sidewalk into the next town as I had every day that summer, an older man in a semitruck honked his horn and smiled at me, and I understood for the first time that I could get attention without having to do anything. And I understood that this was what it meant to be a girl; this is where we had power and meaning in the world.

Stephanie has a similar story. When she was seven, in the first grade, she had a boyfriend. Most all the girls and boys in her class had boyfriends and girlfriends. It was just something they said. It's not like any of them did anything other than hold hands or kiss on the cheek. But for Stephanie, having a boyfriend felt intensely important. She explained to me that she knew even then that if a boy wanted to be with her, it meant something was important about her. Like in all the Disney movies she'd seen, the most handsome, valiant males choose the girl characters, and the girls' destinies are fulfilled through this process. When her boyfriend decided he wanted to be another girl's boyfriend instead, Stephanie was devastated. Her main focus became getting another boy to like her, and somehow she knew that to be liked—even at seven—she had to be physically attractive, maybe even sexy. Stephanie told me she feels like she never had a chance, that her narrative about boys making her worthwhile began so young that she has no idea who she might have been otherwise.

It is easy to see how genuine sexual desire gets submerged within each girl, even lost. In conversations with adolescent girls, researchers have found that girls will not speak spontaneously about their own desire; rather, they will only speak of their own desire in terms of relationships. In the educational psychologist Deborah Tolman's research, she found that even when asked directly, many girls don't quite know how to answer.[15] They note that it isn't something they discuss. They get angry. They giggle. They say they don't have those kinds of feelings or that they don't want them. Or some of the young women note that girls just don't feel desire in that way, unable to claim an "I" voice on the subject. Those who will finally speak about their desire only do so when they feel safe enough to do so, when they can trust that their words will not be manipulated.

Sexual desire for anyone doesn't exist in a vacuum. Indeed, desire is very much a socially constructed experience, and our society is not keen to include teenage girls in a discourse about sexual desire. We quickly divert such conversations into discussions of virginity and abstinence-only education, the perils of teenage pregnancy, or girls as sexual victims. Certainly all of these topics are valid, but nowhere do we have a means for girls to direct the narrative of their own sexual desire.

I can't help but imagine a society in which girls are allowed this sort of direction. What would it mean for girls to look inward to their talents and strengths and uniqueness, rather than at billboards and television shows and magazines, to find out who they are sexually? What would it mean for girls if they could define their passion through internal avenues of desire? Imagine a girl able to express herself sexually with a boy, unconcerned about how her body looks or whether he thinks she's sexy. Imagine a girl who trusts that when she does express herself in that way, boys will respect her as an equal partner and the rest of her community will celebrate her strength and passion rather than judge her as a whore.

If we are to break down all the reasons we aren't there yet culturally, we must first look at why girls aren't permitted to have this freedom. For a girl, sexual feeling itself becomes tied to being looked at. Without any cultural guidance about sexual desire, we can only ascertain that we must look a certain way to even have sexual feelings. Well-known feminist author Naomi Wolf notes: "Men take this core for granted in themselves: We see that, sanctioned by the culture, men's sexuality simply *is*. They do not have to earn it with their appearance. We see that men's desire precedes contact with women."[16]

Women's desire does not always come before that of a man's desire for her. We know, in fact, that women's sexual desire is often dependent on being desired. In a *New York Times Magazine* article about female desire, the psychologist Marta Meana determined that "women's desire is not relational, it's narcissistic. It is dominated by the yearnings of 'self-love,' by the wish to be the object of erotic admiration and sexual need."[17]

In other words, a women's physical arousal is in direct relation to how much she is wanted—gazed at, one might say—by another. It is difficult to imagine how such desire is not at least somewhat culturally created, how it is at least partially, as Wolf suggests in her quote, tied up with a sense of permission—it is safe to be a desiring woman now that someone else has suggested I am acceptable.

Charlene is a good example of this. She grew up in a tough neighborhood. She watched her single mother scramble to pay the bills. Her father was long gone. She had one sister who was four years younger, so she didn't feel like she had anyone she could relate to. The first time she felt a boy look at her with longing in his eyes, she knew it was something to pay attention to. She spent the greater part of her teens "boy hunting," she said. She wanted to feel that she was desired, because at home she felt so completely undesired. When she felt sexual desire, she told me, it was entirely about that fantasy. If some hot guy with status wanted her, she got turned on and couldn't help herself from having sex with him. The feeling, she said, was intoxicating, because those were the only times her body felt alive with desire, which made her feel alive, period.

These false beliefs—"I'm not good enough, pretty enough, thin enough, quiet enough…"—are one of the defining features of girlhood. For loose girls, sex and sexual attention become the answer to these beliefs. They possess the potential to make us good enough, pretty enough, lovable enough. This is why promiscuous behavior for a loose girl doesn't end in adolescence. It often grows into an addiction of sorts. We try and try again to make the sex mean something about us. But ultimately it only harms us further.

Often, too, teenage girls' experience of desire is subverted and redirected into narratives about male attention. This might be partially due to hormones, but certainly it's also a result of cultural expectation. Genuine sexual desire is lost inside the power of getting that attention. The influence of this, the heady control of getting a boy or man to look our way, to desire us, is perhaps the easiest way for girls to feel any kind of influence when it comes to their sexuality. In a culture where girls' genuine sexual desire is shrouded in silence, where there is no language of ownership for girls' own sexual feelings, it is easy to see how girls gravitate toward this kind of power.

Like Faith at the swimming pool, a girl's sexual maturity must be something of a paradox. Look, but don't look. Touch, but don't touch. In this way, being a girl is invariably tied up with need and negation, and with how a girl must negotiate those opposing forces.

For boys, it is entirely different.

Chapter 2

BOY CRAZY
The Fantasy Girls Have about Boys

*Everywhere I turned there was a new one. I can remember
my boyfriend coming to see me [at college] for the first
time, and I came rushing up from another boy's dorm room
having just had sex, only to then have sex with him.*

Kelsey was always jealous of boys. In grade school she wanted
to be Batman or Spider-Man during recess, but she had to be
Batgirl or the girl being saved. She developed early, with breasts
in the fourth grade. Both boys and girls teased her regularly. They
called her "Chesty" instead of Kelsey, and most who used to be her
friends turned on her because they didn't want to be associated with
her. She cried often, which didn't help, and she begged her mother
to move to a different school district.

In fifth grade, she began to develop crushes on boys. They were
all boys she knew she could never have, but still, she made up elabo-
rate fantasies of them pulling her aside and telling her they secretly
loved her. She imagined them kissing her, how their lips might feel

on hers. And she imagined them offering to take her away from her life, to live just the two of them on an island where it didn't matter if kids went to school.

And in sixth grade, when one of the cashiers at the Burger King down the street from her house suggested she meet him in the bathroom, she did so willingly, feeling that finally someone might want her. He lifted her shirt and kneaded her breasts, and then he told her to jerk him off. He didn't kiss her once. He didn't even ask her name, but he wore a name tag: Greg. She said she will never forget his name. He was her first sexual experience, her first understanding that boys could do something for her, something no one else could. Even though Greg never asked her into the bathroom again, even though she felt rejected and confused by what had happened, the experience set her on a search she is still stuck inside—a search for boys' attention. She has since given blow jobs in stairwells at school, had sex in boys' parents' cars parked in driveways. She has had anal sex with a friend's nineteen-year-old brother. None of them has tried to have a relationship with her. None has fallen in love with her. None of her fantasies about what boys can do for her—save her, release her, love her—has come true. But at sixteen she can't seem to stop. At sixteen, boys still have the only solution Kelsey can see to her feelings of being undesirable.

Kelsey's story is painstakingly familiar. I too spent much of my life believing a boy could save me from my pain. I too felt irrepressibly drawn to boys. I too couldn't help myself. There was something about them. Sometimes, still, I can feel it: boy crazy. Other girls feel the same way. Here are some quotes about their own stories from some of the girls I interviewed:

"I felt like a shell of a person that only came alive when a boy or a man noticed me. I felt like the whole world revolved around being noticed and wanted by a boy or a man."

"My experiences with boys feel like obsession, like there's nothing more appealing in the world."

"I get completely gaga over boys."

"Without a boy in my life I feel like I don't exist."

"What is it about boys?"

Yes, what is it about them? This is the question that drives this chapter. My sense is that whatever "it" is, the groundwork begins young.

Lately, my three-year-old son has been playing make-believe. He wraps a cape around his small shoulders and builds a castle out of his oversized blocks and imagines stories for himself. In all the stories, there is someone he has to save, and in every scenario, I've noticed, that someone is a female. I have no idea where he has learned this narrative. I try steadfastly, albeit unsuccessfully, as his mother to prune out any books or television shows or movies that involve such a relationship between boys and girls. I work hard to speak of boys and girls as equals. But the narrative of a girl needing a boy to save her, and a boy coming along to do just that, is so insipid in our culture that it slipped into his very young consciousness without my knowing.

In truth, it is easy to see how it happened. In even the most innocuous movies—beginning with the ones meant for children—if a boy looks at a girl, if he finds her attractive in any way, it becomes clear quite quickly that he is in fact in love with her. Not only is he in love with her; he has eyes for no one else. And if he loved her as a child, when they grow up, they will be reunited, usually in some way that involves him rescuing her, and he will *still* be in love with her all those years later. And then add to this that so many images of girls—in these movies and elsewhere—show them overly concerned with what boys think of them.

And that is just the media. Beneath that is the very real cultural truth that boys simply have more freedoms in our culture. Boys can take up physical space. Whereas girls must rein in their desires, sexual and otherwise, boys can allow their legs to fall open when they sit; they can yell out the car window at girls walking along the sidewalk; and when they chase girls for sex, they are acting like "typical" boys. For these reasons, boys become appealing to girls on yet another level. Heterosexual girls are drawn to boys physically and emotionally, but they're also attracted to the self-determination and lack of restrictions that boys are allowed in our culture. Studies show, in fact, that girls who adopt the "feminine" role—sociability, empathy, and greater passivity—do not feel as good about themselves as girls who take on more "masculine" traits, such as independence, aggression, and assertiveness.[1]

So it makes sense that girls might find ways to latch on to boys. Boys have something we want: real freedom. Since there has been no way for girls to harness this freedom, they have learned—sort of smartly, I'd say—to harness boys, the owners of that freedom, instead. And this is where the "bad boy" comes in. We all know who the bad boys are. They are charming, generally unconcerned with us, disinterested in any sort of commitment. They are sexy as only things that we can't truly have are sexy. And they are dangerous. Girls are taught early on to stay away from these boys, the ones who will give them freewheeling experiences, including—perhaps most especially—sexual desire.

Jackie lives in Los Angeles, where it's very easy to find what Hollywood considers attractive men. The first time Jackie and I spoke, she asked, "Did you find that you always had to have extremely good-looking men?" She described the kinds of men she always sleeps with. They are B-list actors and models she meets in clubs. I had heard of at least half the men she named or had seen them on television or in an advertisement. She told me she has a crush on a well-known performer. My first reaction was to say that many people fantasize about celebrities, but she and this man had actually exchanged smiles and stares on numerous occasions in L.A. nightclubs. As our conversation continued, I began to understand that this was Jackie's normal experience of men: Jackie was only pursuing men who were out of her league. When she expressed heartache that one of the guys hadn't called her again after sex, it seemed obvious to me that it wasn't because he thought she was unappealing or unlovable in any way, which is what she thought. In my mind, these men were unlikely to date "normal" people. They would have sex with noncelebrities, sure, but they weren't going to have lasting relationships with them.

Jackie is an intensely smart woman, so I was fascinated by her inability to see the way she continually set herself up to feel bad about herself. It struck me that Jackie liked them "unavailable." She liked the thrill of scoring someone so unattainable. It was part of the high. At the same time, though she wasn't aware of it then, she chose unavailable men so when they left she could falsely reestablish her understanding of herself again and again: she isn't good enough. She isn't lovable.

Also, Jackie's B-list celebrities give her an opportunity to express her sexuality in ways that wouldn't matter as much with mere "mortals," as she jokingly calls the rest of the men in the world. If the celebrity boys want her, then she can latch on to their desirability. She ups her status as a sexual person with such bad boys.

For a girl, sex is dangerous. It is a motorcycle ride; it is rushing carelessly along a highway, heading somewhere, hair wild in the wind. On that motorcycle is the man who takes her on the ride, her arms wrapped around a firm, protective chest. That kind of wild, carefree sex is everything a girl can't have, unless she is willing to become a slut. Unless she wants to become potentially unmarriageable, unworthy of respect. Sex *is* that bad boy. Naomi Wolf in *Promiscuities* writes, "The demon lover's tendency toward chaos and escape and risk and selfishness may be seen as a projection of inadmissible female longings onto the male—a way of safely handling and vicariously experiencing the release of women's own wish sometimes to be 'out of control.'"[2] No wonder bad boys are so appealing to so many girls! No wonder they will do whatever they must to get inside that experience with such a boy! For her, sexual feeling is only allowed in the presence of a boy who can contain her, who will take responsibility for the wildness and loss of control. Boys become the stand-in for everything she can't do herself, and she winds up playing out all her drama, discovery, and passion in her relationships with those boys.

A girl doesn't need to feel sad or lost or hurt to become a loose girl. She simply needs to want freedom, to want the wingspan that will let her live her desires. This, I suspect, is why plenty of girls I interviewed suffered through so many of the same feelings but didn't have loveless childhoods. At the core, loose girls are a cultural problem. Yes, difficulty at home can exacerbate looseness. Yes, abuse and molestation make the problem much, much worse. But the bottom line is that girls get attached to boys and male attention because our culture allows boys the sorts of freedoms girls want.

Fourteen-year-old Lourdes met her last boyfriend at an underage club. He was twenty-four, hanging out there with a few of his friends who seemed younger than him. She said there was no question that he was leering at all the teenage girls, but rather than being turned off, she found this provocative. She saw it as daring on his part. He danced with her and then offered to drive her home. After that she saw him every day, but she had to hide it from her parents because of his age. He picked her up from school and would take her back to his apartment that he shared with a few other guys, and they'd have sex. At home, Lourdes's father drank and went into rages. Lourdes and her younger sister had to hide in their room with a chair against the doorknob until he had passed out. She'd made the mistake of getting in the way of his rages before, and she wound up whipped by his belt. Her mother, who was a devout Catholic (or, as Lourdes called her, "a religious freak"), never did anything to intervene. Instead, during her father's rages, Lourdes's mother cried in the kitchen and spoke to God in Spanish. "You know," Lourdes said, "helpful shit like that." Lourdes just wanted out of her house, but she also felt guilty because she didn't want to leave her sister alone with her parents. She thought many times about getting pregnant. She knew for a fact that her father would have kicked her out (and her mother would have just cried and talked to God in Spanish).

Eventually, she and her boyfriend broke up. He moved on to some other young girl without even telling her. She was pretty upset, but she went right back to the club, hoping that some other guy would come along. She says that she has her sights set on someone saving her from her life, and who better to do that than an older guy?

Two-thirds of girls younger than age 18 choose sex partners who are close to their age, and a mere 7 percent choose partners who are six or more years older.[3] But men older than high school age account for 77 percent of births among girls age 16–18 and for 51 percent of births among girls age 15 and younger. Men older than age 25 father twice as many births with teenage girls than do boys younger than 18.[4] So, while teenage girls partnering with older men is not a significant trend, when it does happen, it seems that girls wind up with older men as the fathers of their children.

Why do some girls want older men? A few of the girls I interviewed told me they felt that teenage boys were immature and that they liked how the older men treated them, referring to dinners and gifts. One noted, "It doesn't hurt that they have cars, too." It does seem that girls who like older men gravitate to their money, but research also suggests that girls who choose men so far out of their age ranges also tend toward low self-esteem and depression.[5] Many of these girls are looking to replace their abusive or difficult families with new ones. They often perceive the men as white knights who will save them from whatever pain they're suffering at home.

Regardless of the girls' claims, men who choose teenage girls tend to be immature and insecure, with egos matching those of teenage boys.[6] Many have criminal histories, so they are not the safe havens girls make them out to be. Of course, partnering with a teenage girl under the age of consent is statutory rape, not to be taken lightly.

Grown men who choose adolescents as sex partners tend to have these immaturities, but they also simply learned about girls from our culture. They, like all boys, learn from media that girls aren't worth more than their looks and their accessibility for sex; they absorb this message as completely as girls do. Boys erroneously learn, just as girls do, that boys are horny and girls aren't, and that it is up to the girls to protect their morality by fending off boys' advances. They learn that boys choose girls, not the other way around. And they learn that the more girls a boy can score, the more manly he is.

It is easy to see how these messages can lead boys to behave badly, to try to get girls in bed and dump them just as quickly, to not feel any sort of responsibility for their sexual behavior in the world. It is also easy to see how we don't vilify or shame boys for their sexual behavior the way we do with girls. That double standard is still entirely alive and well. Although it might seem that boys get away with murder in this respect, the truth is that—just like girls—they get pigeonholed away from real intimacy. Our culture's expectations regarding sex harm boys, too. Boys learn that they should want sex, pursue it, and be good at it. They don't, however, learn about the emotional potentials that come along with their desire, and they don't learn that most boys share a similar awkwardness and curiosity, along with the excitement and awe, when it comes to sex. In *Real Boys: Rescuing Our Sons from the Myths of Boyhood*, William Pollack argues that boys' ravenous sexual appetites are more often than not a cover for their fear of sexual humiliation.[7]

Imagine, if you will, boys and girls exploring sexually and safely in a loving, kind way. Imagine they could learn about how to have relationships, could communicate about their needs, without cultural and parental shaming. Sad how much this vision seems like an impossible dream. Before we can look more closely at ways to rectify this, let's examine the role of the girl more closely. After all, as boys are boxed into being owners of their sexual identity, girls are given very few options about who they can be when it comes to sex.

Chapter 3

THE UNHOLY TRINITY

The Virgin, the Slut, and the Empowered Girl

I am still desperate for male attention, and I feel unwanted,
ugly, and needy. Sometimes, I don't like aspects of my
personality. Why am I so selfish? So loud? So unfocused?

THE VIRGIN

Winnie told me she was *never* "that girl" in high school. She was
a virgin. She promised herself she would wait until she fell in love
because, she knows now, her culture had promised her that this
would get her what she wanted. She'd be loved. She'd be valued.
She'd be good.

When she got to college, though, she decided one night she
didn't want to wait anymore. She wanted finally to be "put on a
pedestal," something she had ironically been promised she would
get if she stayed a virgin. But what she really got as a virgin was in-
visibility. The girls around her who were putting out were the ones
getting talked about and pursued. All this time had passed, and she

had hung on to her virginity and still didn't feel loved, or valued, or even necessarily good. What she felt was empty.

So one night she drank tequila and lost her virginity to a random guy. After that, as the weeks and months passed, she moved on to the next guy—and the next, and the next. Winnie says that she had underestimated the intensity of the high that she would get from the attention. She never had guessed how easily promiscuity would become a sort of addiction for her. Today, she says, she's still a loose girl, and she's so deep in it, she doesn't have a clue how to get out: "I still haven't been loved. I still give it away. I still feel empty when it's over."

While promoting *Loose Girl*, I was invited to appear on a morning show with three teens. They embodied the three sexual paths that girls can follow in our culture today: the virgin, the slut, and the empowered girl. In other words, girls can choose not to have sex; have sex but be shamed for it because it's too much, or the wrong kind, or because it harms them; or have sex because they are trying to claim it as their own choice.

Believe it or not, the virgin was the girl who interested me most. The conviction behind her virginity drove her to tell fellow teen girls to retain their virginity. She was 100 percent sure that she was right. And she had proof! Most everyone in the audience lauded her. Her mother was so proud. Sex education—funded by abstinence-only programs—supported her. In fact those programs sent her to talk at other schools. The churches let her know she was doing the right thing. She was a good girl.

The virgin owns a mythic narrative that goes like this: She is more desirable to our culture in every way than the girl who has sex. She is lovable. She is girlfriend and wife material. She is prettier, cleaner, holier, and just all-around better than the girl who has sex. We say that virgins "respect their bodies." (Although this is a concept that always has seemed misguided: Why does not sharing oneself intimately and physically with a partner mean respecting oneself? Why does respect equal denying one's own physical pleasures?)

The virgin myth also assumes that girls have a much lower sex drive than boys, that they don't want sex. It assumes, in fact, that girls are responsible for fending off boys' out-of-control, aggressive libidos. (You can see how easily this notion leads to the deduction that girls can be responsible for their own rapes: "If you dress in sexy clothes, boys can't control themselves," or "If you let a boy kiss you or get sexually excited in any way, you shouldn't be surprised when he can't help himself, even as you say 'no'").

In this way, virgins are assigned a false strength. The virgin teen who was to be on television with me, as well as girls holding the title of Miss Teen America and other spokespeople for abstinence, often comment on how they believe they are stronger than those girls who "give in" to their sexual urges or need for attention. In other words, a girl's strength comes from doing nothing, as opposed to from actually *doing* something in the world, such as being a powerful athlete or saying truths that are unpopular but necessary. This is especially troublesome because it also suggests that there is no possibility for healthy sexual exploration. In this scenario, all sexual activity equals giving away one's power. There is no possibility that a girl can have sexual experiences and still be powerful. Having sexual experiences renders girls weak and helpless.

Most important, though, the virgin myth emphasizes the idea

that a girl is only worth as much as she's able to keep her legs closed. Forget compassion, honesty, integrity, or kindness. As Jessica Valenti notes in *The Purity Myth*, "For women especially, virginity has become the easy answer—the morality quick fix. You can be vapid, stupid, and unethical, but so long as you've never had sex, you're a 'good' (i.e., 'moral') girl and therefore worthy of praise."[1] She notes that this view is just one more way that we value women most for their bodies and sexuality, and for what they do with those.

We even throw virgins parties. In the past decade, we've seen the growth of "purity balls." At such events, begun as a Christian response to rising teen pregnancy and STD rates, adolescent girls pledge their virginities to their fathers until they will wed, and fathers vow to protect their daughters' chastity. There is white cake, exchanged vows, and a first dance, just like at a real wedding. Regardless of the creepiness of twelve- and thirteen-year-old girls having commitment ceremonies with their fathers, the key point is that the balls don't work. Out of a study of twelve thousand girls, those who had participated in purity balls had the same rate of STDs as those who didn't pledge their virginity, and 88 percent break their pledges and have premarital sex.[2]

In so many ways, these sorts of ceremonies set girls up for failure. It might be easy for a twelve-year-old girl to say she won't have sex before marriage, but three years later, she realizes how much she likes boys and sexual experiences. Or as her brain develops further, she begins to think, *Wait a minute. How come I can't have pleasurable physical interactions and boys can?* (After all, where are the mother-son pledge balls? Good luck finding one.) Or, even more likely, she comes to know that her value as a girl is tied up with whether boys want to get with her, and to get boys' attention, she will need to be sexy, and—well, combined with the fact that sex and attention feel good—you can see how easily those pledges become a distant, silly fantasy.

This is not to say that a girl choosing to stay a virgin isn't a perfectly acceptable decision for a teen girl. But so is choosing to have sex. The girls are not to blame here. It's the abstinence train, the co-opting, once again, of a girl's control over her own sexual choices.

That societal pressure to be abstinent has resulted in issues way more dangerous than a girl choosing to have sex: the pressure to exclude information about birth control in sex education and the refusal to supply condoms to sexually active teens. When girls don't know enough about how to keep themselves safe, when they don't have easy access to the very things that make them safe, then we're complicit in the fact that they are unprotected from STDs and pregnancy. If we, the adults, are responsible for our teens' physical safety, then we are failing them in this way.

Equally important, the abstinence train has denied us this discussion around teenage girls and sex, and it has indirectly contributed to why many girls—the loose girls—use sex as a means of self-harm. When we tell girls sex and sexual feelings are bad, when we tell them *they* are bad when they act sexually, they will believe us, and they will use it as a way to punish themselves on their own. If we make sex subversive, then we shouldn't be surprised when girls use sex—something that should be, that *is*, perfectly natural—as though it were fraught with as many dangers as alcohol. And we shouldn't be surprised when they wind up furious and hurt by the way our culture betrays girls in this way again and again.

THE SLUT

When Julia was twelve, her parents divorced and her mother moved them to a small town in another state so that her father would have no access to them. In her old school, Julia had a group of friends. But Julia didn't know anyone at the new school, where the kids had been classmates since preschool. During the days, she walked through the halls, clutching her books to her chest, her head down. She had never thought before about her weight—she was just a little heavy—because she and her old friends hadn't concerned themselves with that. But here, girls called her "fat." Once, while she was at her locker, a boy from one of the older grades stuck his hand out and touched her breast through her shirt. Just like that. She stopped what she was doing, paralyzed. She couldn't breathe, the heat from the place he touched spreading across her chest and into her neck and face.

At thirteen, she found a friend: Audrey. And Audrey didn't care what the other girls thought. She was a year older. They met after school and smoked cigarettes in Audrey's living room. Audrey's parents didn't care. Audrey introduced Julia to beer, too, and sexy clothes, and she introduced her to boys. They went to the movies and came on to the older local boys, boys already out of high school, boys who were eager to take Julia's large breasts and ass into their hands. She was eager, too. Eager for their attention, for what felt like caring, maybe even like love. Later, when they left, often not even taking her phone number, she felt like garbage, like the nothing she believed she really was. But she went back again and again, chasing that feeling.

It didn't take long for Julia to be labeled the school "slut." Every school has one. The slut is so well known that she's become an archetype—a product of a Jungian collective unconscious—as Emily White noted in her book *Fast Girls*.[3] The slut is always the same: desperate, dirty, curvy, asking for it. She is all desire, all sex. She is as bad as a girl can get.

The narrative of the slut has been repeated so often that I almost don't have to note it here. She has sex with lots of boys. She teases lots of boys. She wears sexy clothes. She will do anything boys want her to do. She gives blow jobs, hand jobs, rim jobs. She usually has big breasts. And everyone knows she is a slut. In fact, they are the ones who named her. White noted that when she interviewed girls, this slut myth, the belief in the slut as a real thing, was so powerful, so all-encompassing, that it overwhelmed any of the women's stories.[4] I had the same experience with the girls I interviewed. They called themselves sluts, "blow-job queens." They joked about being amazing in bed, how they perfected their techniques.

They joke, but the truth beneath the myth is that these girls hurt. Virgin, slut, or (as we'll soon see) empowered, all are limited by the outlines of their role, but none is as harmed by her title as the slut, for society heavily and thoroughly ostracizes the slut. Put any celebrity slut's name into a Google search—Britney Spears, Lindsay Lohan, Paris Hilton—and see the parents who rally against them and the endless blog writers who are disgusted by their behavior. Girls in middle and high schools exclude one another from their cliques with that label, reminding one another what is acceptable behavior or not. Parents don't allow their daughters to dress in slutty clothing, fearing that doing so means that their daughters are indeed sluts. Even in horror movies—all the classics, such as *Friday the 13th, Halloween,* and *A Nightmare on Elm Street*—the promiscuous girls are always the first to die.

Milburn High School in New Jersey made headlines in 2009 when thirteen- and fourteen-year-old girls were put on a "slut list." Every year a group of senior girls created a slut list of incoming freshman girls, including degrading comments, such as, "I'm so desperate and hairy that I'll give you drugs for free if you get with me." More shocking to me was that this story made news. Ask your daughters: some equivalent humiliation of girls, because of their sexuality, takes place at plenty of schools throughout the nation. One of the girls who cowrote the list at Milburn High even said, "Really it's all fun."[5]

One of the more contemporary examples of highlighting the school slut is "sexting," sending dirty electronic messages and/or revealing photos or videos through phones. Thirty percent of all teens have reported sending naked pictures of some sort through their phones, and 17 percent of recipients admitted to passing that photo along to others.[6] Most any girl you talk with will tell you that she regrets sexting for that reason—she never meant for the message to get around (see chapter 8 for more on sexting).

Fourteen-year-old Fiona thought that she and Brian were girlfriend and boyfriend, or at least that he was her friend. They had been having sex. It wasn't either of their first times. She decided one night to send him a picture of her naked torso. She wasn't dumb. She had heard about what could happen to photos like that. But she honestly trusted Brian. At least that is what she said, crying, to her best friend, after the photo made its way through the school. In just one day, most everyone had seen the picture, and Brian acted like he didn't even know her. She had never regretted anything more. Over the next few months, much of the school ostracized Fiona, calling her a slut. Boys approached her to ask for sexual favors, and when she tried to ignore them, they high-fived one another. That was a few years ago. Things have since settled down, but Fiona doesn't think she'll ever feel safe around these classmates again. Fiona asked me outright, "Why are so many kids so cruel when it comes to this stuff?"

Amanda, who is now in her twenties, has a slightly different story. She didn't do anything back in high school, she feels, to earn the label of "slut." She just had a lot of energy and verve, which she thinks, looking back, got misinterpreted for sexual energy. Unlike many girls she knew, she didn't get quiet and submissive when she hit puberty. Her mother worked hard to keep that from happening. Her mother spoke loudly about what she thought. She gave Amanda books to read about puberty. She took her to festivals that celebrated girls and their power in the world. At the same time, though, Amanda's mother didn't have great boundaries when it came to this sort of education. She had sex with her boyfriends with the bedroom door open when Amanda was home. She had parties—where everyone shared their art and poetry and music—that sometimes turned into orgies. And, again, Amanda was home.

As a teenager, confused and aroused by all this activity around her, Amanda imitated her mother. She dressed like her mother did with low-cut tops and long, flowing skirts. She took off her shoes in class so she could be barefoot. She wore no makeup and let her hair dread. When she spoke, she did so loudly and with passion, just like her mother. And she did things that were shocking to her classmates, such as pulling a breast out of her shirt and shaking it at a boy or dancing provocatively on the school green. Her classmates didn't understand her at all, and because there was some expression of sexuality in her oddness, they branded her a slut. When Amanda talks about it now, she gets teary and angry. She feels irreparably scarred by that time in her life. She's furious still at her mother for being so inappropriate and narcissistic, and at her classmates for being so insensitive and cruel. She's also furious at herself for not having learned the rules about womanhood the way everyone else seemed to at the time—don't be different, don't be loud, don't have passion.

If nothing is more frightening than a woman's desire, then a young girl's desire is even more horrifying. We ostracize because we are jealous; the slut is the one getting all the male attention. Or we ostracize the slut because we want to protect our girls, because there is some sense that all sex-related behaviors for girls will lead to harm. Or we ostracize simply because we are afraid of what feels different and unfamiliar. Whatever the reason, when we banish the slut, more often than not it's the punishment that harms her, not her behavior.

In fact, if she embraces her behavior, it can earn her a different label. Where for years no one wanted to be called a slut, more recently, being a slut can be a self-proclaimed badge of honor. Meet the "empowered" girl.

THE EMPOWERED GIRL

Seventeen-year-old Ramona wrote me this: "All my family knows about my sexual history since I got expelled from two schools. They have taken me to three shrinks, and I see one every week. They disapprove of my sex life, but now if they forbid me to go out, I'll sneak out as I used to. In the city I live, many men from different countries come to visit and all my friends and I have a list of nationalities we kissed and had sex with, and I'm winning of course. I've had thirty-two different nationalities and want to have more. In four years I have had sex with fifty-six men. I know I'm taking risks and the number is terrible for my age, but I'm not the only one or the worst. I just like having sex."

Something new has entered the culture of women. Lynn M. Phillips, in *Flirting with Danger*, calls this the "together woman discourse," in which women are "sassy" and free in their sexual agency, but in actuality, that "freedom" is limited to a heterosexual stance, one that aims to attract men.[7] In *Female Chauvinist Pigs*, Ariel Levy refers to it as "raunch culture," a culture in which some women have co-opted what men think is sexy and made it supposedly empowering.[8] She includes such examples as *Girls Gone Wild*, pole-dancing lessons, striptease marathons, and women who buy *Playboy*. Tied up with this is the idea that being a slut is a good thing. It means you're strong, in control of your sexuality. The notion starts in the right direction—women can own their sexuality—but it's almost as if, more often than not, women fall back into the familiar tire grooves of what men desire about women's sexuality.

Certainly, this empowered-girl culture has invaded adolescence as well. Thirteen-year-old girls proudly extol their abilities to give blow jobs, which they do in the bathrooms at parties or at school. Middle and high schoolers have sex parties. Girls compete with one another to dress as slutty as possible. In *Unhooked: How Young Women Pursue*

Sex, Delay Love, and Lose at Both, Laura Sessions Stepp notes that, in our hookup culture, teenage girls have abandoned dating and courting altogether and are simply engaging in sexual acts with others.[9] They don't have to want to be boyfriend and girlfriend. They don't have to even like each other.

This may sound empowered, but think about how it would be perceived if such a girl didn't have a male partner, or at least didn't attract one, or if she gave off the vibe that she needed a man. Would she be seen as empowered—or pathetic? Such sexual behavior smacks of the same intentions Levy identified in her interviews with women about raunch culture. If girls have no interest in boys beyond getting their attention and giving blow jobs, then what exactly are they getting out of the arrangement other than the reputation that comes along with it? If they don't *need* boys' sexual attention, why are they competing for their attention? How exactly is this empowering for them?

The month before *Loose Girl* hit the bookshelves, *Marie Claire* published an interview with me about the book. The interview noted what I've come to call my "number," which was forty-something. I had slept with some forty-odd boys and men during my loose-girl years.[10] Soon after, one of the *Jezebel* bloggers posted about the interview. She wrote that I was just another person who felt I earned the right to have a memoir when clearly I was just like any other woman. She noted that forty men was not very many at all and that plenty of women had many, many more men. How dare I try to make money off the fact that men didn't want more than casual encounters with me, as though that were something I experienced and no one else did. And she made it clear that I could not be both a feminist and a person who had had sex mostly because I felt badly about myself.[11]

Two hundred fifty-six comments came next. Grown women said things like, "40 men? I've had that many men in a month. Where's my book contract?" They did the math and determined that I had only slept with two men a year, which by no means gave me the right to publish a book about promiscuity. "How dare she call herself a slut!" one of the women wrote. "You want a slut? I'm a slut!"

Girls and women like Ramona, and like these commenters, carry pride about their sexual behavior, similar to the sort of studly pride we see in boys. A proportion of our culture, tired of the old double standards about sex, have begun to say, "We can have sex because we want to!" Put another way, "We can have sex like men! We can treat our sexuality like men treat theirs!"

Certainly, I agree with this motive, and oh, how I wish we could. But as Levy argues, empowerment in the form of stripping classes and posing for risqué spring-break videos means using the same degrading method a patriarchal society has used to control women to degrade oneself. I would argue that handing out blow jobs like candy could be defined the same way.

"Let's not kid ourselves that this is liberation," Erica Jong said to Ariel Levy. "The women who buy the idea that flaunting your breasts in sequins is power—I mean, I'm all for that stuff—but let's not get so into the tits and ass that we don't notice how far we haven't come. Let's not confuse that with real power."[12] That power would surely include some sense of ownership over our sexual identities; it would surely include girls' understanding that sexual desire lives in them, not in boys' attention to them. Lynn Phillips adds that this notion of empowerment "supports an illusion that young women's supposed autonomy and entitlement somehow insulate them from the possibility of victimization," which explains the anger at *Jezebel* over my sense that, for the most part, my experience with sex had sucked.[13]

I can't assume anything about how Ramona really feels. Perhaps she truly does enjoy her conquests. But while I applaud the idea of a girl going out there and doing with sex whatever she damn well pleases, I don't quite believe that such an achievement is uniformly possible. As Jong suggests, we have much too far to go. Our society is still much too steeped in a double standard about sex for me to believe that anyone, particularly anyone so young, can exist so entirely outside cultural expectations. Also, girls having sex with whomever they want, whenever they want, and without the desire for anything more, seems, like Levy noted, to be a little too close to men's fantasies about girls and women. I'm not convinced that this should be the primary model we put forth for women's sexual freedom.

REAL EMPOWERED GIRLS

Let's imagine what empowerment might look like regarding females and sex. Girls and women who wanted casual sex, not love, would be accepted and respected. In fact, girls and women would want casual sex because it would be understood that wanting sex without strings is a perfectly honorable thing for a girl to want on the basis of where she is in her life. It makes sense for a teenager or young woman in her twenties, for instance, to not want the intensity and sometimes burden of a relationship because she wants to focus on other, more important things: personal exploration, travel, career building, and more. Likewise, if she wants to have sex only with someone she loves, then that's honorable as well, just not more so than the other choice. An empowered girl wears what she wants—she can show off her breasts if she wants to, but she certainly doesn't have to for her to be sexy. She doesn't need to lift her shirt or participate in wet T-shirt contests to be sexually powerful. She doesn't need to have a long list of conquests.

Empowerment has nothing to do with these things. Sexual power is always about a woman's—and a girl's—core sense of herself as a desiring, desirable being whom she is entirely in control of. She decides who touches her and when. She decides how much to share her body or not. And no one else has the right to dictate what that says about her, or to shame her, or to silence her. No one else gets to say, "I'm good at this, but because you do it differently, you aren't." That, my friends, is empowerment.

THE LOOSE GIRL

A loose girl is not empowered. She doesn't secretly want to be a virgin. And she's not just a slut, although she probably embodies some truths behind the slut myth. She falls between and beneath these archetypes, the ones our culture has told girls they can be as sexual creatures. The loose girl has so completely lost herself and her desire in her other wants that sex has become a way to control others, to try to make them want her. And because that authenticity in her relationship to her own desire is so skewed, she almost never gets what she really wants.

For many, many years, I knew that I had a relationship to boys in my life that I didn't understand. I knew there was something about the way I felt about them, how they made me feel, something about how I had used them in my life, but I couldn't make sense of it. Nothing in the world spoke directly to what I felt, to the particular way in which I struggled. Yet at the same time, almost every girl who came into my therapy office, almost every grown woman I knew, had those exact same feelings. We had spent our lives desperately pursuing boys or believing entirely that a boy would save us from whatever pain we felt. We searched each room, each party, each sidewalk, each store and bank and post office, for boys who might give us attention. We made the possibility of our sexiness, our attractiveness to males, a project. We could not work out at the gym without the idea that doing so would get us male attention and, therefore, meaning in the world. We could not try on clothes in a dressing room and not imagine what a boy would see. We cultivated our tastes in music, in politics, in religion, all with the idea that this would make us more pleasing to men. And more often than not, that need for attention had turned into sex, usually sex we wanted, but sometimes not.

More important, we lost our connection to our own desires. In fact, our natural sexual desires had morphed with our desire to be wanted, to be chosen, and—yes—to be loved. We gave up more desires than just sexual ones—traveling, friends, career paths, so many opportunities to be more whole.

Why did it take me so long to understand what had happened to me and to so many others? I read as much as I could, I talked to friends, and I listened to their stories. I wrote and wrote and wrote, trying to find what it was I wanted to say. In particular, I wrote one scene—a scene from when I was twelve and went into Manhattan with my two friends to meet boys.[14] We got all the way there and had to leave, so we tried to get all the way back, but our bus took us only as far as a spot that was ten miles from my house. We went to wait in an all-night gas station, and the attendants there, who were probably in their early twenties, promised to take us home when they were done with their shifts, which would be at five in the morning. On the way home, the guy who drove us reached over and put his hand on my crotch. The first time I wrote that scene, I wrote about the shame and humiliation and hurt. Indeed, that was all true. But I also knew that there was something I was missing, something I wasn't quite getting at. So I rewrote and rewrote and rewrote some more until one day I got to a new understanding, a truer one. Although the scene in that car was one beyond wrong, it was also true that I liked it. I liked the power I felt. I liked feeling wanted and chosen.

When I understood, when I admitted that truth, everything came clear. This was my dirty little secret, the same one so many girls and women shared with me. I had been after something all night. I had wanted this male attention, and now I was getting it. The dirty secret was that I liked it, even as I was ashamed and humiliated, even as I was a victim.

Truths like this one are terribly difficult to find. They are lost inside the noise of our culture that determines who girls are allowed to be. They sit in silence while we struggle to make sense of what we feel. The biggest problem is not that we are silent about teenage girls and sex. Rather, the problem is, as the cultural historian Michel Foucault noted, that we police people—perhaps girls especially—with endless rules about what they can talk about and about what they can claim from their sexuality.[15]

Josie, who is sixteen, identifies herself as a loose girl. When she was little, almost everyone she loved abandoned her. She can't remember a time when she didn't believe that if a guy touched her or wanted to have sex with her, she would be happy and fixed. In the past two years, since she lost her virginity, she has slept with so many guys that she's lost count of how many. She doesn't remember the names of half of them, and probably never knew most of them. Some were friends. She only actually dated one or two of them. Josie says: "I am lonely. There is something missing. Having sex and being in the heat of the moment is a high. And when I'm there and doing it, I don't feel alone anymore."

Guinevere slept with more than one hundred guys before she turned twenty-five. She had the looks and body to attract plenty of men, but, in her words, "I lacked the brains and confidence to use those things to get what I wanted." What she wanted was to be found truly appealing, beyond just her looks. She wanted men to want to spend time with her. She says, "All those years I never realized that given a choice most men or boys will take what they can get whenever they want. I made it incredibly easy for them to get it." She went on to explain the many ways she gave herself away. She didn't make the connection, she told me, between how easily she gave herself away and how lonely and desperate she felt. She was nice to guys, good to them, gave them whatever they wanted. They laughed together; they seemed to like her. But after they had sex, the boys were gone. She constantly wondered what she did wrong. Was she not good enough in bed? Was she too loud? Not loud enough? Was there something wrong with her?

Guinevere's confusion about what boys want is an extremely common feeling among loose girls. They get the clear message from media and peers that boys like sex, that boys like girls who are sexy. But then, again and again, the boys leave after sex. Loose girls almost always assume it's about them—they are simply not lovable enough. There is something horribly wrong with them. They also know the other message that bears down through the schools and Christian organizations: boys don't like girls who put out. So, loose girls shame themselves. The fact that they can't help their neediness, their desperation to be loved, they believe, is surely why boys leave.

Many of the girls I spoke with who identified as loose girls shared with me the ways they acted out in their neediness. They called boys too much. They texted and emailed them constantly. They pushed them away with their desperation. When they tell me these stories, I can see their eyes move to the floor. I can hear their voices drop. They hesitate. The shame they feel about their neediness is much worse than any shame they might feel about their sexual behavior.

Cynthia told me that after the last guy had sex with her and never called again, she texted him five times before he finally wrote back, "Don't contact me again, freak." She spent the rest of the day in bed, unable to move. His words had confirmed for her exactly what she feared was true about her: there was something different about her, something different from every other girl, who seemed to be able to take or leave a guy, whereas once she got a boy's attention, she could think of nothing else but how to make him love her.

Cynthia's dirty little secret is not sex. Like that of all loose girls, her dirtiest secret is her need.

Loose girls come from every walk of life imaginable. They are black, white, Hispanic, Asian, poor, rich, middle class—you name it. Many had great childhoods. Others did not. For some, we can track back to what happened with their parents—mothers and fathers—to get some sense of why they headed down the paths they did.

Chapter 4

BEST FRIENDS AND ROLE MODELS

Mothers and Loose Girls

My mother was my first teacher when it
came to getting men to notice me.

Cicely's family fit all the stereotypes of a normal, nuclear family. She lived with her younger brother, mother, and father in a middle-class home. Cicely's mother had prided herself on making choices for her family that included sit-down meals every night, checking their homework, and always knowing where they would be and with whom. She and Cicely were extremely close, right up until Cicely turned fourteen. That's when things took a turn. Cicely began to want to wear clothes her mother would not allow. She began to sneak out at night to meet boys, then come home with hickeys all over her neck. Her mother tried everything: reasoning with her, grounding her, sleeping in the living room so she would hear whether Cicely tried to escape through the front door. Nothing worked. Cicely, meanwhile, grew more and more resentful of her mother's tactics. She felt increasingly isolated from her family, but got a sense of comfort from her friends, who understood her. Mostly, though, she got comfort from boys, who made her feel special in a way she had never felt before. When they didn't call or liked one of her friends instead of her, she felt devastated, but that initial rush, that feeling that maybe this boy would love her, was worth it all.

Cicely's story is probably familiar to many mothers with teenage girls. Their daughters are precious, lively, compassionate kids. Their mothers know how to reach them. They enjoy their time together. And then all of a sudden something switches. The daughter goes away. She stops communicating. When the mother tries to talk to her, wanting open discussion, the teen gets angry and stomps away. She yells, "You don't understand!" and slams the door. But of course the mother understands. She understands better than anyone.

And yet, according to studies of mothers and adolescents, mothers understand less than they think. According to studies by James Jaccard, Patricia Dittus, and Vivian Gordon in *Child Development*, mothers tend to underestimate their daughters' sexual activity.[1] Most all the girls I spoke with affirmed this pattern with their mothers. Plenty told me that their parents would freak out if they knew the extent of what they did with boys—threesomes and oral sex, for instance. They've hidden hickeys and lied about where they were going and who they were spending time with. One said, "My mother thinks I'm such an angel. She tells her friends how sweet and smart and together I am. It makes me want to puke. She has no idea who I really am."

Much research supports that a healthy mother-daughter relationship is prohibitive of promiscuity among teens. Adolescents' perceptions of their mother's disapproval of premarital sex and their satisfaction with the mother-daughter relationship are significantly related to abstinence for teens, less frequent sexual intercourse, and more consistent use of contraception among sexually active youths.[2]

However, in a survey of one thousand fifteen- to twenty-two-year-old girls and one thousand mothers of teen girls conducted by *Seventeen* and *O Magazine* through the research firm Harris Interactive, only 4 percent of girls claimed that their beliefs about sex were influenced by their mothers, and 40 percent said that talking to their moms about sex didn't really affect their decisions.[3]

All these mixed messages for mothers don't help the already-terrifying process of raising teenage girls. Lydia, a self-proclaimed loose girl, told me that her mother relayed those mixed messages in the home. She walked around naked saying, "We're all girls here." She encouraged her daughters to feel comfortable with their bodies. But she also told them they should not have sex or lead on boys, who would do anything to get into their pants.

"It was confusing," Lydia said. "So ultimately I just did what I wanted."

This sort of disconnect is reflected in the *Seventeen* and *O* survey, where 90 percent of mothers claimed that they'd spoken to their daughters about how to make the decision to have sex, but only 51 percent of the girls claimed to have had the same conversation.

A few things are at work in such numbers. One is that mothers are generally uncomfortable talking to their teens about sex. Following the dominant discourse about girls and sex, mothers talk about the issues involved—pregnancy, abortion, and STDs. Most adolescent girls claim that their mothers don't talk to them about the aspects of sex that they deem more important—such as the emotions involved and the physical feelings. Generally, they feel like they're receiving warnings and rules, and that the conversation is rarely much of a two-way street.[4] One of the girls I interviewed told me that her mother would never even know all the things she wasn't saying; the girl knows that there are certain topics her mother doesn't want to hear about from her, and one of them is definitely her desire to be with boys sexually.

Mothers are uncomfortable partially because sex is such a taboo subject for teen girls. But they've also adopted the social standard that if you discuss sex and sexual desire with your daughter, she'll fall down that slippery slope into promiscuity. As a result, many tell their daughters about abstinence. They let them know that sex before marriage is off-limits. Then they assume (or pray) that the girls will follow their advice.

Girls, too, often feel uncomfortable talking to their mothers about sex, particularly when they fear judgment, rigidity, or attempts to control. But even without those factors, talking about sex with any parent is burdened with embarrassment.

Certainly, this adds to the reasons that one of the more important topics missing from most conversations about sex is masturbation. Letting a girl know—from early on—that it is perfectly fine to touch herself in private is a great way to support her natural sexual feelings without needing a boy. Even the well-known sex therapist Laura Berman said in an *O Magazine* interview about talking to daughters about sex, "It's important to talk to her about having a sense of control and pride over her body, and to let her know there are ways she can make herself feel good before she's ready for sex, like self-stimulation." The interviewer asked, "Seriously? Mothers should talk about masturbation?" Berman replied: "If you want to raise a sexually healthy daughter, yes. That may mean attending to your own sexual health. A lot of women grew up with the idea that masturbation is wrong or dirty." Indeed.[5]

It's not just the conservatives and abstinence advocates who wince at such a conversation. "That is private business," one mother said to me. This head-in-the-sand approach, though, puts a wall up between teen girls and adults. As long as mothers don't talk to their girls about sex, they are setting up a greater likelihood that their girls will use sex to self-harm.

Masturbation is a major taboo, and a long standing one at that. Some of the myths are familiar—you can go blind, you'll grow hair on your palms, or your reproductive organs will fail. Others contain that common double standard—boys masturbate, but girls don't, or girls who do masturbate are hypersexualized, exposed to images or experiences they shouldn't have been.

But the real truth about masturbation is that it's as natural and normal as it can get when it comes to sexual exploration. The larger percentage of the population masturbates, and they do so through old age.[6] In fact, one study suggests that 20 percent of all senior citizens masturbate at least once a week.[7] The joke goes that 98 percent of the population masturbates, and the other 2 percent are lying. Although statistics suggest that men masturbate more than women, I think we can all agree that this is due to both the stigma put on women for having desires and the likelihood of girls' and women's lower honesty in reporting masturbation occurrences, as women are traditionally not accepted for their sexual desires. If girls and women are expected be in love to have sex, then certainly admitting their solo sexual desire is too risky.

The Boy Scouts of America, the Christian Coalition, and the Roman Catholic Church are all vocally opposed to masturbation. Christine O'Donnell, who ran for the Delaware Senate in 2010 (and lost), spoke on MTV in the 1990s about how masturbation was a sin because it was equivalent to committing adultery.[8] In 1994, Dr. Joycelyn Elders, the U.S. surgeon general, was forced to resign from her position because she suggested that masturbation should be a part of sex education. Conservatives and moderates were outraged to the point that Elders left her post.

Meanwhile, when we look beyond opinion and stigma, research suggests that masturbation is an essential part of sexual development, and girls' hesitations about masturbation are correlated with having uneasiness about intercourse.[9] The sex educator Sharon Thompson notes that one of the things masturbation teaches is that all those things we feel happen inside our own bodies.[10] So many girls make all that sexual excitement about the other person. In reality, those feelings are their own creation and they could have those feelings without needing a boy around to feel them. Assuming that girls will develop more confidence about their sexual feelings if they do masturbate, they might also be more self-directed about their sexual behavior. They will likely know better what they want and what they don't. And what better way for girls to acknowledge and attend to their sexual desires without putting themselves in the way of STDs and pregnancy?

So how should mothers address sexual behavior with their girls? Lynn Ponton, author of *The Sex Lives of Teenagers*, created a comprehensive list of considerations, including starting early, before adolescence; being conscious of talking to your children about sex and sexual feeling without mentioning your own; continuing the conversation and communication long beyond a singular talk; and recognizing that your work as a parent is to guide and suggest but not to direct.[11]

If daughters are going to have sex, and we know from the statistics that many will, then mothers should make condoms available to their daughters. We know that adolescents use condoms more than adults do, which means they are *willing* to use condoms.[12] Therefore, parents have a responsibility to keep their children as safe as they can by providing condoms in case their teenagers are choosing to have sex. And parents need to talk with them about condoms early. A study conducted by the Centers for Disease Control and Prevention determined that mothers who discussed condom use with their teenage daughters before first intercourse had daughters who were three times more likely to use condoms than those whose mothers discussed condom use with them after first intercourse.[13]

Another very important issue arises when it comes to mothers and daughters regarding sexual behavior. Many mothers are still dealing with unresolved feelings surrounding their own promiscuity. They either continue to act in loose-girl ways, or they feel anger or pain or resentment about those feelings themselves (see chapter 9 for more about the grown-up loose girl). We know that modeling is one of the primary ways children learn. It doesn't matter what mothers say to their daughters if they don't walk their talk.

Children—perhaps especially teenagers—are hyperaware of hypocrisy. Communication to teens about sex—from media, from parents, from educational institutions—is loaded with mixed messages. Teenagers look perhaps most critically at their parents for hypocrisy and will quickly dismiss a mother's admonishments if she isn't following the same advice. And if a mom is acting out sexually, needing too much attention from men, or even focusing too much on romance, girls pick up those messages more than anything else that might be said.

This is not to say that all loose girls have loose-girl mothers, but having a loose-girl mother generally means that the mother is somewhat oblivious, which won't help her daughter's emotional health when it comes to sex. Research shows that parents who are insecurely attached—meaning that important bonds were disrupted when they were children—tend to parent in ways that pass on that insecurity to their daughters.[14]

Janet and Shawna are a mother and daughter who have lived on their own since Janet and her ex-husband Greg divorced. Janet always told Shawna that she didn't want her to give herself away to just any boy, but when Janet began to date, Shawna felt like she was seeing her mother in a different light. She dressed in sexy outfits. She changed her hairstyle. Once Shawna saw her mother French kissing a date in the kitchen. His hand was squeezing her behind. Shawna felt sick but also slightly aroused. She was happy for her mother, but it also frightened her. She felt like she didn't know her mother at all.

Janet and Shawna's situation is a common one for many teenage girls. Janet isn't necessarily doing anything wrong, but without any discussion, Shawna sees her mother's behavior as hypocritical. There are layers to every story, too, that are harder to see. In that brief anecdote, for instance, you don't see that Janet also had a history of needing men's attention. When she married, that need went into a sort of remission, but suddenly free she found herself craving attention again. In this cycle, Janet will find it hard to be there fully for Shawna. But if Janet can build awareness about her own behavior, she can discuss her tendencies with Shawna. They can talk about how women are made to feel in their culture and how hard it is to fight the current. She can promise Shawna that she will work on this issue in her own life and that Shawna can come to her with any feelings about the process, even unpleasant ones. In other words, Janet doesn't have to be perfect. No parent can be. But she *can* take responsibility for herself and be honest, the two most important things a parent can do.

Hannah has a very different story. Her parents divorced when Hannah was ten, and a few years later, her mother met Chris at a singles' dance. Hannah's mother immediately began to transform, and not in a positive way. Whatever Chris liked, her mother did. For instance, Chris liked high heels, so Hannah's mother went out and bought a few pairs and she wore them all the time. Hannah didn't like Chris one bit. He insulted her father, whom he'd never met. And he insulted Hannah, too. When Hannah would say something back to him—something like, "Excuse me?"—her mother told her to stop it, to not act fresh with Chris.

Every day, Hannah felt like she had to hold herself still, not talk, not express any of her feelings. If she did try to talk to her mother, Chris would show up and give her mother a why-do-you-let-her-get-away-with-it expression. Soon after, her mother would warn her to knock it off. It got so bad, in fact, that Hannah started having occasional panic attacks. Her mother found Hannah shaking uncontrollably in the bathroom one time, and she still did nothing. One time, Hannah said point-blank to her mother, "You choose him over me," and her mother didn't deny it. Now, Hannah says, she tries not to think about it too much. Instead, she fantasizes about having a boyfriend. She told me, "I think of having a boyfriend's arms to wrap me up tight, kiss my hair, hold my hand, and cuddle with. I find myself now looking at any guy, imagining that. I don't find many guys at my school attractive, and the ones that are have personalities that ruin it, or they're into smoking pot, or I just have no way of approaching them. Now whenever I think I like a guy, I don't know if it's just because I'm desperate like my mom or if my crush is genuine. I just want to feel good and have someone there to love me like that. And it doesn't help the way my mom is acting, and what she says makes me think I can't be happy if I don't have a man."

Hannah's mother has tons of work of her own to do before she can be a positive influence on Hannah when it comes to romance. Like Janet, she needs to examine her own issues with men and the ways she has turned to men to fill something in her that she can't fill on her own. Clearly, Hannah's mother has put her own desperation for love above her care for her daughter, something I too commonly hear from teenagers. Unless Hannah's mother puts her daughter's feelings first, Hannah will continue to feel confused about her own impulses when it comes to romance. Hannah has difficulty separating her identity from her mother's, which is typical of a mother-daughter relationship, but particularly one where the mother has no boundaries around her behavior.

Every once in a while, I hear positive stories, too. I know a fourteen-year-old girl named Nel who recently started dating, and one evening she came home with a hickey on her neck. Her mother saw it, let her daughter know she saw it, and told her that she was fine with that hickey. Her concern, she let Nel know, was that Nel was making choices she wanted to make. She only wanted to be sure that Nel felt comfortable with what was happening and that she wouldn't do something she didn't really want to do. At first Nel rolled her eyes and said, "I know, Mom!" But about an hour later, Nel came back to her mother and said that she did realize that sometimes boys wanted to do more than she felt ready for, and sometimes even she wanted to do more than she was sure she was ready for. Nel and her mother wound up having a long, open discussion about how boys are always considered the horny, sexual aggressors, but really there were things girls wanted to do, too. But girls are very aware that if they let boys know they want those things, they quickly get labeled "sluts." Nel and her mother agreed that this was unfair, and together they discussed ways Nel could work her way around this double standard while still staying true to herself, such as by thinking through her sexual behavior before acting, and perhaps even talking to her mother about it first.

Sometimes the media gets it right also. One mother-daughter sex talk that received lots of attention for being honest, realistic, and all-around positive came from the NBC drama *Friday Night Lights*. On the show, the character Tami, Julie's mother, treats Julie with respect, asking her open-ended questions about her feelings and experiences. She also shares her own honest feelings. Here is an excerpt:

Tami: "And you know, just 'cause you're having sex this one time doesn't mean that you have to all the time, and you know if it ever feels like he's taking you for granted, or you're not enjoying it you can stop anytime...and if you ever break up with Matt it's not like you have sex with the next boy necessarily." (She tears up.)

Julie: "Why are you crying?"

Tami: "Because I wanted you to wait...but that's just because I want to protect you because I love you, and I want to make sure nothing bad ever happens to you. And I always want you to always be able to talk to me even if it's about something so hard like this."

Julie: "I didn't want to disappoint you." (Tami shakes her head and hugs Julie.)[15]

A conversation like this one, and like the one Nel and her mother had, is a great example of mothers encouraging and supporting open dialogue about sex while respecting their daughters' thoughts and feelings. In both examples, too, the mothers take responsibilities for their feelings about their daughters' sexual behavior rather than projecting those feelings on the girls. This is a big difference from the kinds of conversations I hear about too often—one in which a mother simply tells her daughter that she should not have sex until she is married, or alternatively, one in which the mother is trying to be her daughter's best friend. When a mother shares too much of her own past experiences with sex, or when she encourages her daughter's sexual feelings as a way of validating her own, she crosses a boundary, one that can feel violating to a girl.

So a balance such as the ones Nel's mother and Julie's mother managed to find—where they remained their daughters' mothers, guiding them and providing safety for the girls while also supporting their daughters' feelings and sexual discovery—is a difficult balance indeed. Mothers have a unique responsibility here, one they must take very seriously as they navigate their ways through the treacherous field of a teenage girl's sexual discovery.

This has been a long-standing stumbling block. My mother's generation had mothers that tended toward silence. They simply didn't speak about sex to their daughters. One day, the daughter's period arrived, the mother took her to get Kotex, and that was it. They were told to not have sex before marriage. The end. Some of the mothers of my generation tried to do things differently, but many went too far the other way, offering too much about sex, breaking boundaries, wanting to share like friends. The mothers of today have still been mostly left out in the cold with this subject, mainly because mothers are women, which means no one has told them that their desire was normal when they were growing up, that it is a necessary part of the equation when it comes to sexual development. Mothers so often feel helpless in the face of this task of guiding their daughters safely through the wild, roaring rapids of adolescent sexuality. They try to tell their daughters what they need to know. They warn them. But such tactics don't work with adolescents, who need to know that their knowledge and beliefs are respected. The most important thing a mother can do, really, is to just listen.

Fathers have their own set of challenges.

Chapter 5

DADDY ISSUES

How Fathers Matter

*I've spent my life trying to replace my dad who had
nothing to give me, who never even tried.*

S arah, now in her late twenties, has slept with seventeen or eighteen guys, all in about five years. Three-quarters of them were one-night stands, and she can't remember all the names or what order they came in. One was a professor in the college she attended. Three or four of the guys were actual relationships that lasted a year or more. Sarah didn't have sex until she was twenty-one which is later than the average for girls (which is seventeen). In high school she was into sports and schoolwork and not so much into boys. She did have a boyfriend her senior year—but she believes she messed that up when she started looking to her best friend, a girl, for emotional fulfillment instead of him. All of this sounds perfectly normal.

But then, Sarah's best friend had sex with Sarah's father. From then on, everything changed. She said, "I like to blame my father and my shitty genes for my promiscuity, but I know this is just an excuse." True, but her father's behavior was also a reason. Sarah has more recently been in therapy because, twelve years after the incident between her friend and father, she still finds that her depression is uncontrollable.

Breanna had a military dad, and his job required him to travel overseas for the majority of her childhood. When she was nine years old, he left again for a one-year tour of duty overseas. A friend's father was known for taking the neighborhood children on camping trips, with and without their parents, and Breanna's mother thought it was a nice gesture, especially since her father was gone. It was on that camping trip that she says she learned about her body and her friend's father's body when he molested her. Her father returned several months later only to tell her mother that he wanted a divorce. The two events, both terrible disappointments and betrayals for Breanna, led her down a desperate path to feel loved by a man.

Stories like Breanna's, and to some extent Sarah's, are the stories we expect when looking for narratives behind loose-girl behavior. We expect loose girls to have problems with their fathers. Why? Well, the assumption is that a girl who seeks attention in men has daddy issues.

A number of readers have asked me whether I've found that the majority of girls who contact me have absent fathers (I haven't). Google the words *girls*, *promiscuity*, and *reasons*, though, and you will find many articles and blogs noting that the reason girls are promiscuous is that their fathers were absent or otherwise unavailable. Fathers don't give girls what they need. They pull away when a girl hits puberty, perhaps frightened of the girl's emergent sexuality or put off by their sudden attitudes. Or they left long ago, a shadow in the girl's life. We assume that girls look for that elusive father figure in other men.

As one preacher writes in his blog:

They will become teen girls and start looking outside the home for what they cannot find inside the home. They will turn to peer boys to meet their unmet need for affection, attention and love... These girls are often abused by boyfriends. This changes their life. And more than 90 percent of all teen girls who get pregnant, report that they did not have a close, loving relationship with their father.[1]

I searched and searched for the source of his statistic that 90 percent of teen girls who get pregnant didn't have loving relationships with their fathers, but I couldn't find it anywhere. This type of lack of evidence crops up repeatedly in discussions of daddy-daughter issues. I don't doubt that it can be a part of the picture, but I fear we tend toward giving fathers too much responsibility for their daughters' sexual lives.

A communications professor wrote in an article on AskMen.com that girls with "daddy issues" exhibit sexual aggressiveness, excessive flirting, and clinginess.[2] Here lies the issue that we've discussed in previous chapters: cultural assumptions weigh down the terms he uses. Girls who want sex are "aggressive," and girls who want more than sex are "clingy." Would we say that about boys? But what's key here is that he provided no real evidence that girls with daddy issues possess these traits. It's just another cultural assumption.

A psychologist who devotes much of her career to actively preventing same-sex marriage writes on her own website (syndicated on a Catholic organization's website):

When a girl doesn't have a father to fill that role she's more likely to become promiscuous in a misguided attempt to satisfy her inborn hunger for male attention and validation.[3]

Again, the author provides no source material as evidence, and her comment is entirely presumptuous. Yet another psychologist writes:

Perhaps the arena in which the most painful process of learning how to deal with the early lack of a father is played out is in that of relationships. If a girl has not been assured of her value as a woman by that early relationship with the father, she finds it difficult to relate to men precisely because she may often unconsciously seek to find that recognition in the eyes of the beloved... and this may lead her down an early path of promiscuity...[4]

Keep looking, and you will find the same sentiment again and again. The actress Megan Fox said that "girls are awful" because they all have daddy issues.[5] And, still, where is the evidence?

The truth is, the idea that promiscuous girls have daddy issues comes directly from Sigmund Freud. He put forth the Oedipal complex, which theorizes that boys unconsciously want to kill their fathers and marry their mothers. Carl Jung then coined the Electra complex, which is the psychosexual theory that girls develop a sexual attachment to their fathers. They carry this attachment into adulthood, always searching to replace their fathers with other men.

The Electra complex has made its way into plenty of literature—most notably in Sylvia Plath's poem "Daddy." We see it in self-help books and movies and television shows. In the second season of *Tough Love*, for example, the matchmaker Steve Ward had the women explore their daddy issues by writing letters to their fathers. The message here is that until the women resolve their issues with their fathers, they won't be able to have healthy relationships with men. Almost all the "slutty" girls on television have absentee fathers—Serena on *Gossip Girl*, Tyra on *Friday Night Lights*, Rayanne on *My So-Called Life*. Girls are abandoned by their fathers and look to replace them with men.

When we finally look more closely at the research, we find that one of the largest predictors of teenage pregnancy and early intercourse is indeed a single-parent home, and most of those homes, of course, are fatherless. (Single-parent households are also correlated with all sorts of risky behavior for children, including alcohol and drug use.)[6] There is also some evidence that fatherless households, or households with marital strife, particularly when the father withdraws, are correlated with earlier puberty, but only in higher-income households.[7] The assumption is that the presence of fathers provides a sort of protection against growing up too quickly, and without that presence, girls might be hardwired to go out and find themselves a protective mate, although that doesn't account for why this seems to only hold true in higher-income families.

A 2003 study was able to find evidence of increased early sexual behavior and teen pregnancy in a group of 242 U.S. teen girls without fathers living at home, but not other behavioral problems, which suggested a causal relationship between absent fathers and sexual behavior. In the same study, 520 New Zealand girls did not show this individualized behavior increase; rather, many behavioral problems increased.[8] But in a study that came out the same year, published in *Child Development*, researchers found that boys and girls living in two-parent homes with irritable, impulsive fathers had more behavioral problems than those living with just their mothers.[9] So, although there does seem to be some evidence that fatherless girls will become more sexual, there's also the suggestion that those with "bad" fathers wind up with behavioral problems.

I certainly don't want to suggest that fathers don't ever influence their daughters regarding sex and relationships, because they likely do. Exactly how, though, is more of a mystery. There are plenty of studies that reveal some sort of correlation between sexual behavior and absent fathers. The problem is that most of what we find seems informed by cultural ideals, which makes this sort of research hard to wade through. For instance, many studies claim that girls are more likely to be promiscuous, but then those studies don't define promiscuity. Do they simply mean that girls seek out more sex? Or do they mean that girls seek more sex that will make them feel bad? None of these studies distinguish the two. They say girls are sexually active, as though that by itself means something negative to be avoided.

Likewise, it's consistently not clear whether the teenage girls in such studies engage in riskier behaviors because there is a father missing or simply because one of their primary caregivers is missing. One study, performed by a researcher who was concerned with the ways prior research was often used to argue against same-sex marriage, looked more closely at the dynamics in a range of families and found that the gender of parents in child-parent relationships has minor significance when it comes to children's psychological adjustment and social success.

Because of these various biases, we can't assume that absent fathers by themselves lead to loose-girl behavior. To say so oversimplifies a complex, culturally cued issue. Certainly, I've found this in my own interviews with various girls. Loose girls—girls who act out sexually in ways that are self-harming—come from single mothers, single fathers, intact families, happy homes, and even experiences of sexual abuse and incest. Whatever type of home you can imagine, loose girls grow up there. All it takes is for a girl to have some sense that she isn't good enough, isn't lovable, isn't right. And that is too easy for a girl to feel when every image reflected to her reminds her that she will never be as pretty as she should, when every message she's given about who she must be to be worthwhile is confusing, ambiguous, and contradictory to the others.

Still, fathers matter to girls, and perhaps it goes without saying that when fathers are absent or abusive or otherwise not present and loving, girls will probably feel they aren't good enough, aren't lovable, and so on. Put a different way, a girl's relationship with her parents—whomever and how many of them there are—matters. And if there's a father in the picture, that father can do things to better ensure that his daughter won't engage in self-harming promiscuity.

Chantal lives in a single-father household, which is how I spent my adolescent years as well. She was close with her father, who was concerned that Chantal would miss having a mother in her life. He did everything with her and her younger brother. He took them camping, to baseball games, to festivals and on road trips. He didn't date, which upset Chantal. She wanted him to find a partner, to have someone he could share with. When I pressed her, she admitted what she really wanted was for him to stop sharing with her. He spent too much time with her, she said, and she wished he would focus on someone else. There wasn't anything inappropriate going on; he just didn't seem to have much of a life beyond his kids and his work, and that frustrated her. "So many of my friends complain that their dads are never around," she said. "I'd love it if my dad were never around. He's a loser."

Chantal is seventeen and has had sex with fourteen guys. When I asked what it is she wants, she said, "Something different. I just want some way out." She began to cry. "I'm scared that I'll never get away from him. It's like he needs me or something. It's gross."

Chantal's relationship with her father—though close and loving—suffocates her. Her story is an example of how the Electra complex isn't solely responsible for girls using sex to fill something inside. It's also an example of how ineffectual a father can sometimes be when he is simply trying to love his daughter. In Chantal's case, she felt her father was too close. As she said, it felt "gross."

In the single-father household I grew up in, my father often commented on women in my presence in ways that taught me what made girls and women desirable. He noted when women on television were pretty. He told me my friend had a cute body. He said he liked to take walks past cheerleader practice at the high school across the street from our home, and he encouraged me to try out for cheerleading, too. He also touched his girlfriend's ass in front of me or made sexual noises when he looked at her body.

My father was the main man I turned to in order to understand the male species. I looked to him for a sense of what men liked in women. My father's immense inappropriateness showed me that men liked girls who were pretty and sexy. He also let me know that men preferred girls who didn't make waves, who didn't need too much. Meanwhile, I needed so much that he wasn't giving me. Because my mother was gone, I needed him to give me emotional attention. I needed him to care about my feelings, to guide me down a positive path. I needed him to listen—really listen—to what I had to say, to not demean my feelings, and to show interest in what I did.

Fathers don't need to be physically absent to abandon their daughters. There are many ways to leave. Many fathers worry about how to negotiate boundaries—particularly regarding physical contact—with their sexually blossoming daughters, but they often set up bigger boundaries than necessary. Some physically withdraw, unwilling to provide affection anymore. Others become more controlling with their daughters. Both reactions set a girl up to feel left out, misunderstood, and treated unfairly.

Many fathers also make the mistake of stepping away from their daughters because their daughters pull away from them first or because they suddenly don't understand who this angry, easily hurt girl is. For many fathers—my own included—girls are overwhelming creatures, so different from boys. Many fathers don't know how to handle them.

My sister's room and my room were down a long hallway, and I remember my father racing past that hallway. It seemed to us like he didn't want to know what was down that hall. He was terrified of us. We exasperated him. Two teenage girls! He had grown up with brothers and didn't have a clue as to how to deal with our outbursts, our needs, and our sadness.

In these situations, though, fathers must find ways to do the opposite. They need to actively engage their daughters, to ask them about their interests, their hopes, and their feelings. They must find ways to push past the discomfort and awkwardness that can at times accompany such interactions. Daughters need their fathers. They need every possible person who might love them—who might care about how they feel or might care what happens to them—to actively show them that they do.

Fathers are likewise in an excellent position to teach their girls about the various ways our culture degrades and disrespects females. They can clarify that they will not treat women that way and that they won't stand for people treating their daughters that way either. They can address how girls are expected to look good rather than do good. They can encourage them to get involved in something that isn't about what boys want from them, and they can support their daughters' talents in sports, arts, and intellectual pursuits.

At the same time, they can be understanding that many of their daughters will want to be attractive to boys, will concern themselves with "typical" girl interests, such as clothes and makeup. They can both be careful to not judge those interests and make clear that what makes their daughters special in the world is who they are, not what they look like. This is a hard one, because every last message girls get from mainstream culture suggests the opposite. Every last message tells girls that they are the sum of their physical parts, that they can tell whether they matter in the world by whether boys like them. Fathers are in a unique position to show them that men can feel otherwise, that girls can be wholly loved simply by being themselves.

An odd response to this effort, though, is the purity ball, which we explored briefly in chapter 3. Purity balls are Christian ceremonies in which girls pledge their virginity to their fathers and fathers vow to protect their daughters' chastity. Girls wear white gowns, fathers wear tuxes, and they slow dance after their vows. But the reasoning behind the creation of these ceremonies might not be what you expect. In a TLC special about them, Randy Wilson of Generation of Light, the Christian organization that founded purity balls, noted that all girls have the same questions: "Am I beautiful? Am I worth pursuing?" He said that fathers needed to answer this question for them so they didn't go out into the world to find out from someone else.[10] While I can get behind the idea that fathers need to be an active part of their daughter's self-esteem, this idea that girls need to feel beautiful—and therefore worth pursuing—distresses me. If fathers focus on their daughter's appearance, just like the rest of the world is already doing, they miss out on the chance to teach their daughters that they are worth pursuing for much better reasons.

Worse, the purity balls drop all the control over who a girl can be as a sexual creature into fathers' laps—into men's laps. The message is this: "Men know what's best for you. Your father decides who you can be sexually." It would make much more sense to me to have mothers and daughters in such ceremonies, where mothers pledge to share their wisdom and guidance regarding sex, and where daughters vow to communicate with their mothers about their sexual exploration.

Janice's story is a good example that shows how purity balls, and the intention behind them, miss the mark on what girls need from their fathers. Her father died from cancer when she was eleven, just as she was in the throes of puberty. She has many positive memories of him comforting her when she was scared, playing games with her, and reading to her at bedtime. Janice's mother was devastated after his death, and Janice remembers those first few years as grief stricken and painful. Her mother was a mess, barely capable of taking care of Janice and her younger brother. But over time, the grief softened, and their household felt less dreary. That is when Janice began to find boys. Her mother started dating again just as Janice did, too, and her mother fell immediately for a man whom Janice didn't get along with. Soon, he became her stepfather, which only made Janice feel lonelier. He was nothing like her father, and Janice didn't understand why her mother would choose him. Janice started hooking up with boys, which was not really satisfying but gave her something to look forward to. She experienced a sort of high, she told me, when a boy turned his eyes to her body and she knew she had some sort of control over him. She loved the feeling of connection, of her body pressed against someone else's, the sense of safety, of solidity. A boy's presence felt like the opposite of having lost her dad. Janice did not want a relationship with any of them. She only wanted those brief moments of connection.

The problem was that she felt awful afterward. Every time they went their separate ways, Janice felt the familiar pain of abandonment. In other words, she craved a momentary sense of intimacy, much like the intimacy she was now missing from her father, but she didn't want the long-term responsibility of a relationship with some boy. Add to this that the boys at her school began to talk, and soon she became known as a girl who would put out.

In college, Janice finally had a chance to start over, but the pain she held in her heart about her father never went away. She felt desperately confused. She still had never had a boyfriend, and she wasn't sure she could ever trust a boy to not leave her, especially after the way they treated her in high school.

Janice's story is an example of how complicated father issues can be. They are rarely straightforward. For Janice, so many issues were at play. The first, of course, is that she lost her father and was left to struggle with her grief in a way for which no one was to blame. Then Janice faced cultural expectations at her high school about her sexual behavior. Over time, this too affected who she would wind up as in relation to boys. Finally, there is the fact that her mother remarried a man with whom Janice felt no connection. Those three wounds entangled themselves inside Janice's experience of herself as a sexual person and as a person who could have a relationship.

Would a purity ball have saved Janice? The question is outrageous enough to reveal how impotent such a solution is for most people. Most girls don't live the fairy-tale lives such a ceremony promises. They lose people, their parents divorce, they are sexually abused, they are made fun of and excluded. When they grow up, men rarely arrive on white horses, like they did for Cinderella and Sleeping Beauty. Men rarely show up at the father's door and offer to take over caring for the father's daughter. And why would we want that for our girls anyway? Why aim to treat our girls like helpless princesses when they can instead relish their competence as surgeons, welders, artists, scientists, and teachers? When they can do something worthwhile in the world, not just look good on someone's arm?

Such an approach has the power to keep our daughters safe from all sorts of self-harming behavior, not just promiscuity. In the next chapter, we look at these other means of self-harm.

Chapter 6

LOOSE GIRLS IN CONTEXT

Risks and Losses

When we broke up, I slept with guy after guy to fill the emptiness that I felt. I started cutting and became addicted to drugs. I became known as either "That Girl That Cuts" or "That Slut."

In this chapter, we look at the prevalence of depression and other mood disorders that coexist with promiscuous behavior. We also discuss some of the other ways girls harm themselves in conjunction with promiscuity, such as alcohol, drugs, cutting, and eating disorders. How do these behaviors interact with promiscuity, and in what ways are they part and parcel of the same thing? We then examine the question of whether loose-girl behavior can be considered an addiction. And finally, we devote a few words to homosexuality in relation to promiscuity.

THE LOOSE GIRL, MENTAL ILLNESS, AND RISKY BEHAVIORS

Seventeen-year-old Gigi has slept with twenty-two boys. She knows her number because she keeps a careful log of every one, noting what they looked like, what she found most attractive about them, and how they dumped her. Many, she said, just never contacted her again. All times, she was drunk. She hated how she felt each time, but she kept going back for more. Then she would lie in bed, numb, unable to move herself for hours. She also cut herself, which she believed helped with the numbness. Some days she didn't leave her apartment and just moved between the bed, where she lay staring at the ceiling, and the bathroom, where she used a razor to cut.

She had a boyfriend once. It was a yearlong relationship that ended badly. The first four months or so were OK, but soon after, things started going sour. They had fights that always ended with her screaming for him to stay. A few times she held his legs, like a child might. She threw things at him sometimes, once narrowly missing his head with a television remote. When he left for good, she tried to kill herself by taking a handful of Advil PM pills, but she called her friend soon after, terrified she might really die. Her friend took her to the hospital, where they pumped her stomach. That was when a social worker came to see her; soon after she was diagnosed as having borderline personality disorder.

One might say that Gigi is a loose girl. She was promiscuous and always felt terrible afterward. She used boys to fill her emptiness. Gigi is indeed a loose girl for these reasons. But her case is more complicated than that. She has a personality disorder, which means that she needs to work on much more than her behavior around guys and sex to feel better about herself. Indeed, personality disorders are notoriously difficult to treat because they are defined by enduring and persistent abnormal behaviors and thoughts. People with personality-disorder diagnoses often deal with the conditions for life.

Janet was diagnosed with bipolar disorder as an adult, which is a mood disorder, considered more treatable than personality disorders. But when Janet was a teen, few people had even heard of such a thing. She was a heavy drinker and pot smoker from a young age. She knows now that those things were a way to self-medicate, to stop the fast-moving, obsessive thoughts that plagued her day and night. She had a lot of sex, too, usually with strangers, and she berated herself for it later. Sex drive can increase a great deal while manic. The problem comes later, when the person—usually a female—realizes she wants more than just sex in her life. Because men are trained to think of women who are easy to sleep with as not relationship material, the sexual behavior rarely turns into more than a night or two.

Add this rejection to the shame people often feel after manic episodes. For women, promiscuity connected to mental disorders is particularly hard. The shame that comes with having a mental health disorder in the first place multiplies the shame that many girls feel about having and wanting sex, and the ways in which they get punished for it through rejection or derogatory labels ("slut" and "whore," for instance). This sort of shame is pretty prolific, of course, when it comes to young women and promiscuous behavior. A culture that finds sexual behavior among young women unconscionable will only further punish girls who have sex because of an unresolved pain.

Gigi's and Janet's loose-girl behavior does not stand on its own; for them both, it's affected by all of the issues that arise from having a personality disorder and a mood disorder. For most loose girls, it's the same: their promiscuity does not exist in a vacuum. Promiscuity is commonly associated with almost every disorder you can imagine—bulimia, attention-deficit/hyperactivity disorder, conduct disorder, borderline personality disorder, and bipolar disorder, to name just a few. Promiscuity in teenagers is also typically associated with adolescent depression. Sexually active girls are more than three times more likely to be depressed than girls who are not sexually active. They are also three times more likely to commit suicide.[1]

Behaviors can compound these conditions. In middle adolescence, we see the highest levels of coexisting behaviors with promiscuity, such as substance use, alcohol use, and arrests.[2] We know, too, that those adolescents engaged in more promiscuity also tend toward more risky sexual behaviors, such as not using condoms.[3] Likewise, with other types of risky behavior, we are likely to find negative behaviors around sex.

Teens fourteen and older are twice as likely to have sex under the influence of alcohol or drugs. Older teens who drink alcohol are seven times more likely to have sexual intercourse and are twice as likely to have four or more partners. Drug-using older teens are five times as likely to have sex and three times as likely to have four or more partners.[4] A Washington University School of Medicine study found that alcohol dependence and conduct disorder contribute to having a higher number of sex partners among older teens.[5]

And a relatively notorious study that came out of a U.K. university noted that women who drank were 40 percent likelier to have abortions—notorious because pro-choice parties were dismayed by the researchers' choice to point to abortions rather than something less politically charged, such as sexual activity.[6] The other criticism leveled at this and the previous study was the lack of attention to the stigmas applied to drunkenness among women and how that relates to abortions or sexual intercourse. There is a long history of the alcoholic woman as an acceptable target of sexual aggression, with more than one court proceeding leading to the "blame the victim" status given to women who drink and then become victims of rape.[7]

Eighteen-year-old Niesha told me she only has sex when she's drunk or high. For her, all the activities together are what she's after. She likes the whole experience, the sense that she can get pulled out of her life, which currently has very little direction. Her parents made her move out the day she turned eighteen, and so she lives with a couple of friends in a tiny apartment. They all work in chain restaurants during the day, and at night they party. They invite some of the guys they work with, who bring fifths of liquor, cocaine, and pharmaceuticals, and they party until four or five in the morning. Invariably, one of the guys winds up in Niesha's bed. It's been a rotating cycle; she sleeps with whichever one gets there first. The next day she is always late for work, with a pit in her stomach about what happened the night before.

When I talked to her, she asked me whether I thought she had a drug and alcohol problem. I told her it sounded as though she were using a number of substances and situations to try to soothe something inside.

Of course, adolescence is a time of risk taking. Most adolescents use these years to experiment with their own boundaries, with what they can handle, and with identity. Promiscuity is, in many ways, a perfectly normal part of that experimentation. But as with substance use, because sexual behavior is stigmatized, many teens turn it into self-destructive behavior. When we see other types of self-harming behaviors in teenagers, we tend to also see sex used in negative ways. This is important, because it describes the difference between normative sex—normal sexual exploration—and sex used to harm oneself.[8]

In almost every email I receive from readers, girls ask me why they can know their behavior hurts them, and yet can't seem to stop. They know they are having sex for the wrong reasons. They know they need something from it that they won't actually get, that they are setting themselves up to feel even worse. There are many answers to why loose girls have trouble stopping the behavior, but an important one to consider is that the behavior is an addiction.

ADDICTION AND THE LOOSE GIRL

I've gotten some flak for using the word *addiction* attached to the idea of loose-girl behavior. While promoting *Loose Girl*, I gave a number of readings from the book with follow-up question-and-answer periods. Inevitably, there was one person in the audience who was unhappy with the fact that I'd suggested that being a loose girl was an addiction. One man said, "I almost died from my addiction. Did you?" Of course, I could have said defensively that I could have almost died from HIV or some STD. I could have died when, as a young girl, I put myself in danger by going off with strange men. But this isn't really the point. That man in the audience was angry because he had surely seen a number of issues showing up lately as addictions: sex addiction, love addiction, relationship addiction. And perhaps he felt that calling these issues addictions took away from his own struggles with chemical addictions.

But these issues are rightfully addiction, too—they are not chemical addictions, no, but process addictions, which is an addiction to an activity as opposed to an addiction to something that is ingested. Process addictions include spending money, gambling, Internet use, and—you guessed it—sex and love. A person with a process addiction is after psychological gratification and will indulge in their "drug" of choice enough that he or she build up a sort of dependency. The danger of process addictions occurs when the activity gets in the way of one's daily life functioning or leads a person to harm his or her body, as with eating disorders. Sex and love addictions are example of pseudorelationship addictions, a type of process addiction, which are so integrated into our society, often considered the norm, that it is tricky to decipher what is truly an experience of addiction and what is simply a bad relationship.

Perhaps it helps to define addiction. Craig Nakken, author of *The Addictive Personality*, defines addiction as an attempt to control the uncontrollable cycles we all experience in our lives.[9] We all experience loss and heartache. We all don't get what we want plenty of times in our lives. But when a person uses a particular object, event, or another person to try to control how that feels, to produce a desired mood change, and when that person *has* to use this thing to feel better, that is addiction.

Those mood changes can also be thought of as intoxication. So when a sex addict experiences an uplifted mood while in a sex shop, that is a sex addict acting out her addiction. Or when a boy looks at a loose girl and smiles, and she winds up forgetting all the other plans she had for that evening so she can focus on making that boy hers, that is the loose girl acting out her addiction. The point that crosses this behavior over to addiction is the loose girl's inability to attend to anything else in the face of feeding her desire. When her life has become unmanageable, to use the language of the twelve-step programs, when she has lost something that ultimately matters more to her, such as a long-term, loving relationship, a chance to have children, a career, she has entered into a phase we can frame as addiction. Or, perhaps put best, when she keeps doing it even though she really, really wants to stop, she has entered the world of addiction.

One way that loose girls are different from, say, girls who are just moving through a phase, or from girls who really want sex and are only troubled because it's not accepted by society, is that loose girls know that what they are doing hurts them, but they can't seem to stop. This is why I classify the behavior as addiction. This is where it is different from healthy sexual behavior. Loose girls don't have sex for the right reasons, or at the least for reasons that will benefit them. They have sex to maintain the addiction, which is the same reason smokers keep smoking long after they want to quit or that pot smokers keep waking and baking long after they've decided their drug use isn't working for them anymore.

Beth wrote to me after coming out of rehab for heroin use. She said her addictions to men and heroin are remarkably similar. If a man rejects her, she turns to heroin to get that good feeling back, and she has spent many months homeless and on the streets as a result. If she is off heroin, she man hunts to get the feeling back again. The pain she feels, she said, is so deep and awful that she cannot stay away from one or the other. She had two years of sobriety from both, after which she felt like she'd really done important work to move on.

She met a man she thought was different. But it turned out he was just like the others in her pattern. He was unavailable, unable to give her what she needed. He treated her like he cared for her, slept with her willingly, but said he wasn't interested in more than friendship. So she wound up on the streets again for seven months. She slept with five random guys, feeling deep pain about the guy who sent her on a bender. She wants so badly to break free, to stop turning to things that hurt to try to get away from hurt. She recognizes the irony. She sees how irrational her behavior is. She knows, too, that she should never talk to that guy again, erase his number, stop answering his texts, but she can't. She feels trapped in the cycles she's built for herself because her only other option is terrible despair.

The object of a person's addiction—the heroin, the drink, the boy, the porn—is always a stand-in for a real relationship. It becomes, in fact, an addict's primary relationship, meaning that the addict finds it much more difficult to have successful romantic relationships. The main point here is that, while those with pseudorelationship addictions desperately want some sort of real relationship, they actively avoid intimacy through their addictions. In general, too, like any other addicts, they head further into their addictions because of the shame and pain their addictions cause them. Every time they prove to themselves that they can't have love, they act out further, digging themselves even further into their inability to have love.

Also, it's important to acknowledge what is beneath the addiction, which is always the kind of tremendous pain and despair we saw in Beth's story. So many addictions are attempts to escape anguish. The more the addict escapes it by pursuing his addiction, the more tremendous and unmanageable that pain seems to be. With chemical addictions, that sense becomes reality because the addict literally changes the brain's ability to feel pleasure. With process addictions, that sense of terror about one's pain is largely a result of anxiety. When a person avoids the thing causing her anxiety, the avoidance becomes evidence that the thing is worthy of feeling anxiety about. It's a sort of circular reasoning we do when it comes to anxiety. In reality, the thing causing the anxiety is rarely as horrible and terrifying as our anxiety makes us believe it is. So, while the pain behind addiction is very real, it is usually not as insurmountable as we feel it is. It might be initially, because it's been unattended to for so long and because it's a new thing to feel it, but over time we desensitize to its false strength.

It is very human, this desire to categorize and label and understand. We've seen a fascination with process addictions in our media over the last decade or so. David Duchovny was one of the first celebrities to admit his sex addiction after playing the role of a sex addict on the television show *Californication*. Russell Brand admits to being a sex addict. Tiger Woods went to a treatment center for sex addiction after revealing his long list of female sex partners while married. Dr. Drew Pinsky produced and starred in *Celebrity Sex Rehab*, which followed a number of celebrities through their rehab for sex addiction (and one for love addiction). Sex and love addicts are also prone to voyeurism and exhibitionism. Although one can imagine feeling tremendous shame while shooting up on-screen, if you're a sex addict, you probably don't mind acting sexy in front of a camera.

This fascination has at times made me hesitant to commit the loose-girl syndrome to an addiction model. It is important to determine what really is addiction and what is shame with respect to behavior that is simply culturally unacceptable. As with everything surrounding teenage girls and sex, the lines are blurry. Our society is so firmly opposed to any teenage sexual behavior, particularly from girls, that it would be easy to say that all sexual behavior is negative and should be treated as addiction. But teenage promiscuity isn't always the result of severe pain or low self-esteem. Statistically, that is more often the case, but as with any statistics, it is important to acknowledge that there is a percentage of girls who develop low self-esteem because of how society judges and punishes them for wanting and having sex.

That said, addiction is often a very real part of loose-girl behavior. The feelings and bad behaviors have lots in common with other process addictions, such as sex and love addictions, but they are distinctly their own thing. We can define the loose-girl affliction as needing male attention to feel worthwhile. Sex addicts are obsessed with sex. They think about it constantly, need more and more sex to reach the same high, and are dysfunctional in their lives because of it. Love and relationship addicts are obsessed with getting love, with having relationships, and they spend a great deal of time ritualizing how to get them and how to keep them. If a relationship is threatened, they focus obsessively and act compulsively to keep the relationship or get it back, and they experience unbelievable despair when a relationship ends. All these addictions include being trapped in a cycle of pursuit and pain. All of them have a great deal of fantasy tied to them, and those fantasies get in the way of being able to have any kind of real intimacy with another person.

Pseudorelationship addictions are also about power and control. Kelly McDaniel, a love, sex, and relationship addict therapist, writes, "Women who become addicted to relationships and sex are escaping not only painful feelings, but the painful cultural inheritance that places them in an inferior position to men. Sexual power can turn the tables."[10] Young women learn to use sex to try to control their relationships, to try to make men like them. Sexual attention is easy to get when you're a girl, so girls often use it to try to make things go where they want, to try to maintain the good feeling that comes from being wanted. One can see how easily that can slip toward sex again and again—how gratifying it feels to a girl to have a boy's attention on her and no one else—even if the addiction is not to the sex. Taken further, one can see how the girl who winds up having sex again and again with random boys feels awful and used.

Perhaps some of this sounds familiar to you. Perhaps you, too, try to heal something inside with a relationship or with a man. Throughout the book, I've noted that it is almost impossible to be a girl in our culture and not feel that way. Everywhere we look, we're told that everything we could ever want, every wish we want fulfilled, will come with a man's love. If we follow this, then almost everyone has the potential to become a love addict. Or perhaps, too, you think about sex constantly, or you use sex to get something else. Since girls aren't permitted in our culture to have sex without wanting love, and since girls want sex just as much as boys do, perhaps you might potentially fit the bill for sex addiction.

My story in *Loose Girl* has been called the story of a sex addict and love addict. When *Marie Claire* published an interview with me, they titled the piece "Confessions of a Sex Addict," which was followed by that *Jezebel* blogger who wrote that I wasn't a sex addict; I was just a typical girl. I absolutely agree. I wouldn't define myself as a sex addict, and I would categorize myself as a typical girl. And if we follow the definition for sex and love addiction, almost every woman has behavior that has at times crossed into love addiction or sex addiction. It is how we try to have control in a world where girls are not allowed control over their sexual identities, their desires. It is how we have power—false as it is—in a world where girls aren't given much power.

For this reason, focusing on the label "addict" doesn't always make sense, nor does unpacking which addiction you have—especially since so many of them overlap. Most love addicts are also loose girls. Most sex addicts are also love addicts. Most loose girls are also relationship addicts. It's not terribly useful to try to narrow down which ones you are. More useful is to examine the addict aspect of your condition, to see yourself as a person with an addictive personality, and to simply note how easily you keep those addictions alive (see the appendix for addiction criteria).

Of course, it might be useful to get diagnoses for some

conditions, especially those for which there are empirically tested treatments. If we have well-researched solutions, by all means, let's use them. But it is also my opinion, after counseling many girls with relationship issues, that most process addictions—including the loose-girl condition—should be treated not as disorders but as culturally cued issues, as should the addictions we developed as a result, which we must wrestle with as we aim for more fulfillment in our lives. We must work with them personally, and we must work with them culturally, meaning that we must work on ourselves, and we must do what we can to transform the culture that sets us all up to be addicts.

LOOSE GIRLS AND SEXUAL ABUSE

Sex abuse and molestation are commonly associated with promiscuity. The assumption is that when children's formative experiences with sex are some sort of violation, they will be unable to have a normal relationship to sex in the future. This makes perfect sense until we address the question of what makes for a "normal" relationship to sex, particularly when we're discussing teenage girls. Is the fact that they are having any type of sex somehow abnormal? I can't help but notice, for instance, as I read through various studies about adolescent boys, that sexual activity is almost never listed as a "problem."

In a meta-analysis (a study of studies) performed in 2001, researchers found a significant correlation between sexual promiscuity and childhood sexual abuse.[11] But when we look more closely at the data, we see again that *promiscuity* is undefined. What does this mean to the various authors of the studies? Does it mean simply sexual activity, which tells us nothing at all? Or does it mean sexual activity that makes the subjects feel like garbage? And do they feel like garbage because of the sexual abuse they suffered?

Many advocates for sexual abuse survivors have argued that this assumption that victims inevitably become promiscuous is offensive. Sexual abuse is a situation in which a person's autonomy is taken away from him or her, and when we make assumptions about the effects of this, we take away autonomy once again. Heather Corinna, owner of the blog *Scarleteen: Sex Ed for the Real World*, notes that she can't imagine that there is any group of people *more* conscious of having sex when they want it versus when they don't than sex abuse survivors. Think about it. When you've had an experience that was clearly unwanted, then you are more prepared to recognize it when it approaches again. She additionally writes:

> *Sometimes survivors do have sex that is compulsive or reactive. We also want to be sure to recognize that sometimes that's about trying to relive the experience to process it or change the script or other unknown unconscious motivations which can be about processing and healing. In other words, even in some cases where it is or appears troubling to an outsider, it may just be where someone is at in their own process, and outsiders should carefully consider the judgments they may make about that, or any way they may pathologize behavior that may not be pathological. Hopefully, people can also start to garner an awareness that judging a rape survivor's sexual behavior can put even more baggage on a person than it can to non-survivors.*[12]

So, while statistics tell one story, beneath the statistics are the more personal stories, the ones that deserve our attention and that might be more accurate than studies. The point here is not that some of those who've experienced abuse don't act out promiscuously; it's that some do and some don't, and we don't always know what's behind people's reasons for having sex. Danger always lies in making quick assumptions about people's sexual behavior, especially when those people are female.

HOMOSEXUALITY AND THE LOOSE GIRL

I realize it's odd to segue into homosexuality here, since being gay is not a mental illness, a self-harming behavior, or a transgression. But in examining the various associations with promiscuity, we must take a look at homosexuality. For years, the gay community has been stereotyped as promiscuous. This association came about mainly in the 1980s, when HIV/AIDS swept through the political and social landscape. Gay men are the ones most associated with promiscuity, and then bisexuals and transgendered people. Many assume that gay women are quick to commit, thus downplaying promiscuity. But homosexual people are just as likely as heterosexuals to want monogamy, or to use sex to feel loved, or to feel shame about sexual desire. The statistics bear out this truth. According to a survey administered in San Francisco, 58 percent of gay men and 81 percent of lesbians are in long-term relationships.[13] Another survey of 156 male couples showed that the average length of relationship was 8.9 years.

Miriam, nineteen years old, has slept with five men and more than fifty women. She grew up as one of eight kids, a middle child, and felt lost in a sea of children at home, no more visible than any of her siblings. Eventually, she grew up and left home. She moved in with a girlfriend who brought people home as "gifts" for them to share. At first, Miriam said, she couldn't believe her luck, but over time she started feeling bad about herself. She needed every woman who came through the house to want her more than they wanted Miriam's girlfriend, which also made her feel bad. Eventually, she started an affair with one of the women. She knew she was hurting her girlfriend, but she didn't know how to stop herself. The other woman made her feel so special, like there was no one like her, which was of course the opposite of how she'd felt growing up. When I asked Miriam if she considered herself a loose girl, she said she absolutely did. Just because she liked girls, she said, didn't change that she had those same feelings, that craving to have someone make her matter.

LOOSE GIRLS IN CONTEXT: A CONCLUSION

Promiscuity is bred among all sorts of mental illness, substance use, histories of sexual abuse, and sexual orientations. It is listed as a symptom of various problems teens may run into. And yet almost no studies have isolated it to learn about how to treat it. Many girls and women who have approached me for help have noted that they've had plenty of therapy in their lives, often for depression, anxiety, or adjustment disorders—a term therapists use when a person comes to therapy for basic life-adjustment issues, such as divorce, empty nest, job loss, etc. But even with all that counseling, they have felt like no one could ever help them or even adequately address their loose-girl issues.

Some of the problem is due to the relationship between the client and therapist. Sexual behavior tends to be underreported because of the sense that talking about sexuality is taboo, particularly across generational differences. If clients bring up transgressive sexual behaviors at all, counselors often assume that the best approach is to get their clients to stop the behavior. Even more likely is that the promiscuity as a separate issue doesn't get attended to: we assume that if we treat the more general issue—substance abuse, depression—then the promiscuity will resolve itself as well. But unfortunately, girls who learn to act out sexually tend to keep doing so until they address the core issues surrounding those actions; usually those issues include a tremendous amount of shame and neediness. And that point—that shame and neediness sit at the heart of loose-girl behavior—is probably the most important one a counselor to a loose girl can know.

Next we look at how losing one's virginity ties in to loose-girl behavior and how loose girls experience continual violations throughout their sexual lives.

Chapter 7

SAYING YES, SAYING NO
Consensual Sex and Rape

I lost my virginity at age fourteen. Really, it was rape.
After that I pretty much gave sex out to whoever asked.

YES—LOSING VIRGINITIES

Sandy, who is fourteen, told me she doesn't plan to have intercourse until she is in love. "That's really the only way to do it," she said. "Right? Because otherwise you just feel bad about it." I asked her what she meant by "feeling bad."

"I mean, everyone will think you're a slut and no one will want to be your boyfriend."

"Doesn't that seem a little extreme?" I asked. "Why would people react that way?"

"I don't know," she replied. "It's just the way it is."

Every girl learns early "The First Time" narrative. There is only one acceptable way to lose your virginity. You fall in love, the two of you decide you want to share your love in a deeper way, you do it, and he loves you forever. Usually, too, this happens on your wedding night. You "save yourself" for him so you can be special and pure, so you can be clean and worthy of him. Girls are taught that their virginity is a gift, one that they should give only to the "right person."

Of course, most girls don't have this experience. As I noted in the introduction, the statistics tell us that half of adolescents and a quarter of early adolescents have had sex, and most have had experiences that are much more complicated.[1] Many—two-thirds of adolescent girls, in fact—regret their first times. Many decide to just "get it over with."[2] Many speak of their first time as "disappointing," because the myth around losing one's virginity, of how special and meaningful it's supposed to be, rarely matches the reality. Many wind up date-raped or lose their inhibitions via alcohol.

Because it is so socially unacceptable for a girl to want sex outside marriage, she will often create fantasies around losing her virginity, such as believing that she is in love or that her relationship with a boy matters much more than it actually does. According to a series of surveys by the Kaiser Family Foundation and *Seventeen* magazine, 50 percent of girls ages 15–17 believed that they would marry their first sexual partner.[3] While boys get the luxury of just trying their damndest to get laid for the first time (laden with their own cultural pressures about losing virginity, of course), girls have to devise rituals around it. They must be in love, or they must do it after a romantic night at the prom. They have to wait for the timing, the mood, the meaning, and the guy to be just right. Some girls tire of this eventually. If things don't line up the way they planned, they wind up just getting it over with. The truth about the first time is that 23.4 percent of first sex experiences are one-night stands, and about two-thirds of U.S. teenagers who've had sex wish they'd waited longer. At the same time, 26 percent of teens think it's embarrassing to admit they're virgins, and more than half believe that their peers think that having sex by fifteen is socially acceptable. Most believe that their friends have already done it, even when they haven't.[4]

So why do girls lose their virginity? Most do so because they are simply curious; they want to know what it's like, and they want to know if they will change in some essential way. So much hoopla surrounds girls and sex that one can see how they would believe that they might be changed. But often that belief leads to disappointment or deflation.

Lola lost her virginity because, she said, she wanted to. She was dating a guy a grade older than her, and her friends were dating his friends. Her friends had already started having sex, so she wanted to, too. Her biggest fear was that her boyfriend would decide he could just find someone else who would have sex with him if she didn't. So, one night at his house while his parents were downstairs, they had sex.

She made him light a candle first—some small part of the romance she figured she needed to not judge herself later. It was, in fact, a detail she always included when she told friends her story about losing it, hoping they wouldn't judge her, too. It was quick, she told me. He used a condom. She didn't feel much pain or see any blood, which had happened to a few of her friends. Then it was done. Afterward, she went to the bathroom and stared at herself in the mirror thinking, *You're not a virgin, you're not a virgin, you're not a virgin.* But she didn't feel any different. Lola had it easy in some ways. She knew she wanted to lose her virginity, and she just happened to be seeing someone who—even though she may not have been in love with him, and he with her—was kind to her and responsible enough to put on a condom.

Lola's story is probably no more typical than a different sort of first time, one where the girl is date-raped, or pressured into it, or drunk. Alcohol is a common gateway to lost virginity, and although some wake up the next day upset with themselves that they got drunk and went all the way, others have confessed to me that they got drunk for exactly that reason.

Nikki told me she got drunk one night because she wanted to lose her virginity. Later on, she wound up puking in the bushes outside her friend's house, but she said there was no other way she could do it without her peers thinking she was a slut. She didn't have a boyfriend, but there was a guy she found attractive, a guy she knew wouldn't go out with her but would definitely have sex with her if she said that's what she wanted. So, she did exactly that. She got drunk enough to go right up to him and say, "I want you." They went upstairs to a bedroom, and she lost her virginity to him. The next day, her friends felt sorry for her that she been taken advantage of. They supported her as a victim. I was the only one, she said, who knew the truth.

In chapter 1, we examined the idea that girls tend to associate sexual desire with being desired. A curious twist to the disallowance of desire is that in our culture, girls are permitted to want sex if love accompanies it. They cannot want sex without it, lest they be sluts. I've heard often from girls that their initial masturbatory experiences involved stories about boys wanting them—her hand on her crotch was a boy's hand, a boy who tenderly loved her as he also

enlivened her sexual arousal—whereas boys' stories of first mastur-
bations usually include images, something they saw, or something
they might do to someone else.

Because of this need for real love to be involved, sex among
teenage girls often "just happens." They get drunk and black out.
They dissociate from their bodies. Alcohol is an easy out, a way not
to take responsibility for one's actions, sexual or not, boy or girl.
People say, "I was drinking—I didn't know what was happening,"
or "I have no control over myself when I'm drunk, so if I did it, it
was the alcohol, not me, making the choice." Alcohol has long been
a regular gateway drug to sex. Often, boys take advantage of drunk
girls, thinking that the drunkenness gives them license.

But many girls, like Nikki, admit that they get drunk to loosen
up sexually. They get drunk because a drunk girl doesn't know what
she was doing and therefore can't be a slut. In my interviews, many
let me know that they used alcohol often as a sort of lubrication, as
a way to open themselves more easily for boys' passes. One noted,
"If I could blame it on the a-a-a-a-a-alcohol [referring to a Jamie
Foxx song] I could get away with anything I secretly really wanted
with a guy."

Jessica told me that when she was as young as twelve, she
started drinking because she was unhappy with herself. It was a
way to be someone else, she said. Someone who could hang out
with friends and not constantly compare herself to them, who
could be around boys she liked and not feel fat or ugly or unappealing. Pretty quickly, too, she learned she could be flirtatious
and open with boys in a way that got her attention, which turned
quickly to sex. She liked the attention and the sex. She liked finally

feeling like she could attract boys, like she was comfortable in her skin. That wasn't the problem.

The problem was the way she was treated the next week in school. Everyone knew. She was called a "whore" and a "slut." Friends started excluding her. At first, she became depressed. She drank more. She had more sex, just trying to feel better. One morning, a friend who hadn't deserted her said, "Jess, you've got to stop drinking. It makes you do stuff with boys, and that's why everyone's being so mean to you." Her statement was like a lightbulb for Jessica: "It was the alcohol. She could say it was the alcohol."

And sure enough, the next time someone made a mean comment about her being a slut, she laughed and said, "I've got to stop drinking! I have no idea what I'm doing when I do. Cuervo is making me a slut." The girl, who had once been her friend, laughed too, and over time they were friends again. Jessica learned the powerful lesson that it is OK to be sexually active with boys if you're too drunk to have chosen to do so.

Sometimes, too, girls find ways to dissociate without alcohol. A young woman told me about her first time with a stranger twice her age, a man she met on the Internet. "He came over one night and he popped my cherry. I was so scared, but big girls, mature girls can't be scared, so I blacked out. I completely blacked out." Another said, "I can't even remember the things I do with boys. It's like the time disappears. Is that weird?"

Maybe girls want to have sex. Maybe they want to lose their virginities. Maybe they even just want to be sexual beings. But without a culturally acceptable avenue to act in such a way, they often feel they have to be blank—not there—in the process.

Drunk, they can avoid the emotions that come along with the cultural weight of having sex for the first time, and they only have to feel bad about it the next day, when it is too late and the deed is done. Girls rarely feel in charge of their own desire when it comes to sex, and certainly this starts with their first time. It's easy to see why girls might revert to choices they later regret, and it's easy to see why they often don't know what it would even mean to feel "ready."

Some may wonder, then, whether I think there is an age or developmental passage at which point I think a girl is officially "ready." But the answer to whether a girl is ready to have sex is entirely individual. Judith Levine, in *Harmful to Minors,* shares one of my favorite stories: a thirteen-year-old girl asks her mother how she would know when she was ready. Her mother replied, "When you want it so much that you feel you can't not have it." She went on to note that sex changes the way you feel about the other person, and that once you do it with that person, you can't undo it or unfeel what you felt.[5] This mother honored her daughter as a sexual being. She told her to listen to her own desire but also to recognize that there are emotional consequences to sex. If only all teenage girls could receive the same advice about losing their virginities, my guess is that a lot more girls would feel in control of their sexual lives.

NO—THE MANY FACES OF VIOLATION

Jennae was raped during Hurricane Katrina. While the rest of the country was terrified about the children and the dogs and the levees and the homes and all the people lost, Jennae experienced her own, very personal devastation. It was easy, sure, because no one was looking. It was easy because everyone's eyes were glued to the television, or making plans to get out, or gathering in the Superdome. It was easy because Jennae just lay there, unsure what else to do. No one was around. She didn't think anyone would care. She had already been called a slut at school. She had already had sex with seven guys, the fourth being her boyfriend's best friend, who she hadn't really wanted to have sex with, but he came into her bed one night, and she didn't know how to say no. That was a violation, too, of course, but Jennae would say it wasn't. Or she wasn't sure. Because every guy she slept with she sort of wanted to, or she liked the attention, and a few she really wanted to, so she wasn't sure how to separate the two—rape and not rape, violation and not violation.

But this time, it was surely rape, because she is almost sure she said not to. She's almost sure she tried to push him off. She can't be sure. They all run together sometimes—the one she really liked, the one she didn't know if she liked but thought she could, the one she definitely didn't want to have sex with. They had all led up to this moment for Jennae. The boy had come by because she hadn't evacuated with her family because she had been fighting with them, and she had said she could handle things herself. He wasn't violent, but he was intentional, forceful. He didn't even try to kiss her. He was from her school. He knew she was a slut. And with her panties off, she saw that she couldn't really handle herself. She knew in that moment, her head to the side so she wouldn't see his face, that she wouldn't handle anything again.

Jennae's story is heartbreaking, and not just because she was raped. It's heartbreaking because violation for her, like so many other girls, was a thing without clear outlines. The sex she had with boys before her rapist was also violating—maybe. The lines remain unclear because how she felt regarding sex, her intention, what she wanted and didn't want, have all long been blurry. Jennae is typical in this way. Like any other girl, she received all the confusing messages about sex. She had normal sexual desire. She got something from sexual attention that was both easy to get and hard to get elsewhere.

Danita told me about how she came to be a loose girl. A neighbor boy molested her when she was eight, and ever since then, she has felt unable to connect in the ways she wants with a boy. She said, "I like sex. Who doesn't like sex? But it's like every time I try to be close with a guy, I feel like he wants to push me where I don't want to go. I don't want to tell them I was raped. It's, I don't know, a turn-off for most guys. So usually I just go along with things, even when I'm not that into it." When Danita met someone she really liked and got into a relationship with him, she stopped wanting to have sex. She didn't want him to touch her, which confused her. She said, "After all those times I had sex, I couldn't understand why I would suddenly feel sickened by sex with someone I wanted to be with."

These experiences of having sex when you only sort of want to, or even don't want to, is one of the defining qualities of loose-girl behavior. We have sex because we want something from it that has nothing to do with the sex itself—in Danita's case, it's the assurance that the guy will still want her, that he won't go away. It's so hard to say no when you feel like a boy's desire for you means so much about you, when you believe it will make you worthwhile. Add to this the fact that boys' sexual aggression is generally considered a normal part of their sexual development—boys will be boys, and they can't help themselves. The end result is usually a sense of violation, much like the violation a person feels after rape. Once Danita got comfortable and safe with a man, her body finally reacted to that violation. She shut down.

Beatrice asked me outright how to say no. She felt like she needed a script—a polite set of lines she could follow each time—so she would stop having sex with men she didn't want to have sex with simply because they wanted her to. We came up with a few responses she could feel comfortable with, including white lies about why she couldn't: "I have to get up early tomorrow," "I'm not feeling well," "I have a boyfriend." Some may judge her for the white lies. People may think Beatrice should simply say, "I don't want to" and leave it at that. Of course she should be able to do that, but she didn't feel ready. Saying "I don't want to" meant they wouldn't try again. It meant she would have to let go of the idea that their wanting her mattered in a larger way. She wasn't at a stage in her recovery where she could do that yet.

The law defines rape as forcible sexual relations with a person against that person's will. Seems simple enough. But nothing about sex—and particularly sex among minors—is simple. Thirty-three percent of sexually active teens aged 15–17 report that sexual activity moved too fast in their relationships. Twenty-four percent have engaged in sexual activity that they didn't really want to do.[6] And in a study published in the *Journal of Sex Research*, of all the times committed couples aged 18–24 had sex, only one in five of those times did the coupling include desire.[7]

In other words, women had consensual sex much more often than they actually desired the sex. In an essay titled "The Not-Rape Epidemic," Latoya Peterson notes all the ways she and her friends have been "not raped" in their lives and how that has harmed them. For example, how many times do girls walk down the street and get catcalled by grown men? How many times do girls have sex because they want to be liked, or approved of, or loved? How many times do girls lie about their ages to men and then wind up having sex with them?[8] As we begin to think more deeply about the complications regarding teenage sexual behavior, the language of rape clearly becomes inadequate.

I certainly experienced this ambiguity myself. I wanted to have sex, sort of. But the desire I had for sex was so completely submerged beneath my desire for attention and love that I couldn't be sure if that were true. Every time I had sex, I had no sexual agency, no sense of my own sexual desire. Instead, my neediness controlled my sexual choices. In this way, I had no sexual self, no self that wanted to have sex for sex's sake. If there was no clear sexual self, then how could I consent to anything? I had absolutely no connection, no consciousness or awareness about the part of me that might want in an unadulterated way to have sex.

In truth, few girls have access to that sexual self. The sexual self is buried deeply beneath all the ways we have worked culturally to keep girls from having a sexual consciousness. Lee Jacobs Riggs writes in an essay:

I let him touch me, never saying no, never saying yes, never probing too much into what his on-and-off girlfriend knew or thought about it. At the same time, I reclaimed the word "slut," told my friends it was good, I wanted it. I excelled at giving blowjobs because I had wanted to excel at something.

Who knows what I wanted. I know that I had a need to assert myself as a sexual person to a world that had tried to erase that part of me that I felt so significantly. I know that I didn't want him, but I did want something.[9]

I heard the same sentiment from many of the girls I interviewed. They too had acquaintance rape experiences—they thought. They too hadn't necessarily wanted to have sex with most of the boys they had had sex with—they thought. The uncertainty I heard again and again is suggestive that many girls—all girls, not just loose girls—don't have access to a part of themselves that might know what it wants regarding sex. If you don't know what you want, how can you articulate clearly what it is?

The age-of-consent law, which is the state-by-state determined age by which point a girl is allowed to consent, was established to protect young girls, but it's easy to see how it furthers the notion that until a girl reaches the age of consent—usually sixteen or seventeen—*no* consent is acknowledged. Before that age, she is the victim of statutory rape. So, for example, a girl who is fourteen may date a boy who is seventeen. Their relationship might include all the typical excitement and feelings of love and drama found in teenage relationships. But if they have sex, mutually consented to in their minds, the boy can be convicted of statutory rape, and the girl can be left with confusion about this idea that she's been "raped." If she understands, as most girls do, that rape means she was forced against her will, how will she reconcile her feelings about her boyfriend and this "fact"?

The law puts forth that same denial about teenage girls having sexual desire. The problem with that, of course, is that teenagers have sex. You can tell them not to all you want, but they have the same biological urge you and I do, maybe stronger, and they don't have the developmental perspective to control their impulses as well as we do. Then add to that the girl who believes that if she says no to her boyfriend, he'll find someone else who will have sex with him, and add to that the girl who wants a boy's attention and knows this is how to get it.

Consent laws have a solid purpose to protect girls when they are truly victims, but legally designating an entire group of people as unable to consent to sex is maybe not the best way to protect girls from having sex that adults don't want them to have (I should note here that an example of a girl truly being a victim, in my opinion, would be when the male counterpart is twenty or older, and the female is fifteen or younger; in such a situation there is undoubtedly a power differential at play). The Netherlands has a great example of how to use such a law to protect rather than silence. There, sexual intercourse between people aged 12–16 is legal, but victims who were coerced or forced and need the law's protection can opt to use the statutory consent age of sixteen to prove that a violation occurred. Also, parents can overrule the wishes of a sixteen-year-old, but only if they make a convincing argument to child protective services.[10] An example of this might be if a fourteen-year-old girl were in a verbally abusive relationship with a seventeen–year-old boy, but she was too blinded by her feelings for the boy, or too scared, to see that. Her parents could then employ the consent age of sixteen to press charges against the boyfriend if they can prove the verbal abuse. This law views young people as capable, thinking, self-contained people who can reasonably make decisions for themselves. So, while teenage girls in the Netherlands start having intercourse much earlier, the country also sees some of the lowest teen pregnancy birth and abortion rates (approximately one in one thousand births) and STD rates in the Western world, which gives evidence of their increased levels of contraceptive use.

If we compare a girl from the Netherlands and the United States, we can see how this might happen. A fourteen-year-old girl from the Netherlands may make a mutual decision with her boyfriend to have sex using contraception. A fourteen-year-old girl from the United States may want to have sex with her boyfriend but knows she's not allowed, so she sneaks it, too uninformed to use protection because no one taught her about sex, thinking her too young. She puts herself at risk of pregnancy, and she likely winds up feeling ashamed.

If we are going to teach girls to say no, we also need to teach them how to say yes. As Riggs writes, she never said no, but she also never said yes. As long as we don't even give girls the option of saying yes, as long as we don't believe we can trust them with their own sexual feelings, we are setting them up, to some extent, to be raped. Look at it this way: if a girl can't separate sexual desire from desperation, if a girl wants attention from a boy because she's told she should and then experiences that wanting as sexual desire because she has no other discourse for sexual desire, then she will not know what she wants. She will not be able to consent or not consent, because she wants something; it might be sex, if sex will get her the love she's after or the attention she hopes for, but it might not be. So she goes ahead and has sex, but later she feels awful because she realizes she didn't want sex or didn't get what she wanted from the sex.

As we have discussed, girls are trained to have boys pursue them. Or, more accurately, they are trained to want to be pursued. But when they are pursued, they are told they can only say no.

Sue-Lin explained to me that, since she was about twelve, grown men have stopped her on the street and outright asked her to date them. She believes they think it's OK to ask her so blatantly because she's Asian. "Men tend to believe we Asian girls are submissive and here to please them," she said, noting a common, racist stereotype. She usually just ignored them and kept walking or said she had somewhere to be. Once, though, when she was fifteen, one of those men followed her—she hadn't noticed—and violently raped her in an alley near her apartment building. She knew the second she saw him that he was angry she had denied him, that she'd had the gall to refuse his pursuit. Sue-Lin's story reveals a twisted result of a culture that can't tolerate a girl having the wherewithal to say no—or yes.

Jill Filipovic explores this connection between gender norms and rape in an essay. She writes, "The message is simple: Women are 'naturally' passive until you give them a little bit of power—then all hell breaks loose and they have to be reined in by any means necessary. Rape and other assaults on women's bodies…serve as unique punishments for women who step out of line."[11]

Once women are raped, their punishment doesn't end there.

A common stereotype about rape is that girls who get raped wind up becoming loose girls. They compulsively pursue sex. In other words, women who have been raped are presumed to be unable to have normal, consensual experiences. Though certainly this might be true for some, it is also not true for others. The important point here is that it is one more way victims of rape are denied ownership over their sexuality—first by the rapist, then by the cultural assumptions about them.

Are victims of sexual molestation promiscuous? The answer is yes, and also no. One out of four females experiences sexual abuse by the time she reaches eighteen, and that includes only reported cases.[12] We've known for a long time that sexual abuse is related to higher rates of depression, anxiety, increased sexual inappropriateness, drug use, and alcohol, but more recently, researchers have looked more closely at these findings and discovered that there is a distinction between those who pursue sex after the abuse and those who avoid it.[13] Some victims use indiscriminate sexual behavior to cope with the pain, others have learned that saying no doesn't matter, and others develop sexual interest too early in a manner that ultimately confuses them. Characteristics of the person who was victimized also affect whether that person becomes sexually precocious or whether she avoids sex altogether, both as ways of coping with the abuse. But family support helps protect against promiscuity among those who've been sexually abused. (Interestingly, family context had less effect on those who didn't report a history of abuse.) Studies have shown that when mothers believed their daughters and took proactive measures to help protect them, girls tended to experience less negative effects.

One of the more interesting findings is that sexual abuse victims are more likely to use drugs and alcohol in relation to their sexual activity,[14] surely as a way to cope with the sexual experiences, which also might explain their increased likelihood of multiple partners.

Lena was raped during her first week at college in her dorm. She was drunk and underage, so she was too terrified to report it. Soon after, she fell into a depression and experienced enough suicidal ideation that she had to leave school. Her mother, desperate and at a loss, found her a psychologist with whom she spoke for the first time about being molested as a child by her youth pastor. It had gone on for two years, and the worst part for her was that she had liked it. She realized through her counseling sessions that she drank so she could have intimacy with people. Otherwise, the shame she felt was too powerful. And that the depression she experienced was from shoving that shame far down.

As we've seen, shame controls so much of girls' sexual lives, from losing their virginity to being raped. It is the common denominator that interferes with healing and recovery, and the one that holds girls away from a sense of their own sexual identity.

Rapidly increasing technology keeps providing more opportunities for sexual behavior among and violation of girls. In the next chapter, we examine what happens to girls' sexual identities online.

Chapter 8

BRAVE NEW WORLD
The Loose Girl Online

I have a Pavlov's dog–reaction to the sound of a text coming in.
I immediately think, "Could it be someone who wants me?"

Fifteen-year-old Johanna sends text after dirty text to boys. She has never actually had sex with a boy, but she knows the language that goes along with it. She tells boys what she wants to do to them, and she tells them what she wants them to do with her. Her favorite part is how the boys always beg her to say more. In real life, boys don't give her that sort of attention, so she loves it. It is the one time she feels sexy and powerful.

On a regular night, she has about five boys she "sexts" with. A couple of times she has sent pictures of her breasts, and once she sent a photo of her entire naked body. She knows full well that pictures can really get you in trouble, though, because a friend of hers sent a photo to her boyfriend, and he proceeded to send it to half their grade's boys. Recently, she's also begun having cyber-sex: she goes online to a chat room to talk dirty with a random user. She loves the power, loves the sense that boys want her. Like many girls, she learned about cybersex at a slumber party. One of the girls knew of it—perhaps from an older sibling—so they found a site online, made up a character, and tried things out. They shrieked when they obtained the interest of someone and then collapsed in hysterics on the ground every time they came up with something new to say. But Johanna remembered that party a year later when she felt unwanted and ugly and had developed crushes that were never reciprocated, so she went back to the same site and got a rush from the power that came with having a random stranger want her, even if the random stranger could easily have been another teenage girl. Like role-playing in video games, cybersex is a way to try on a persona who girls can't be in real life, not without serious repercussions.

Johanna is part of the 39 percent of teenagers who have sent racy messages via text and part of the 20 percent who has sent nude photos.[1] The largely held assumption is that our teenagers are in a whole new world when it comes to sex, and regarding technology, that is absolutely true. The current generation is the first one to have so much immediate technology at their fingertips. Flirting looks different now. Bullying and rumors have a new weapon.

Parents and school officials are scared, and our often frantic concern about kids being exposed too early to sex through technology makes some sense. According to Child Trends Databank, the proportion of children with home access to computers has steadily increased to more than 90 percent as of 2009, and 93 percent use the Internet. According to a 2009 survey of eight- to eighteen-year-olds, 36 percent had a computer in their bedroom, and 71 percent of them also had a television in their bedroom.[2] We know that porn is readily available to most Web viewers. One need only click the button that says "yes" to the question that reads, "Are you 18 years or older?"

As part of this fear, a number of states have criminalized the sending and sharing of nude photos, like the ones Johanna sends, hitting teenagers with child pornography and sex offender charges. As of this writing, at least twelve states have introduced legislation to prohibit or deter sexting. State laws range from minor dings on a juvenile record to child pornography convictions. Each state controls the severity of its laws about sexting, and school officials and parents of girls who've had their pictures distributed bring the most charges.[3] The question is, What really happens to girls who use this sort of technology?

Media concerns itself, of course, with the sensationalized, fear-inducing stories, such as the one about Jesse Logan, the eighteen-year-old Ohio girl who hung herself after a nude photo of her had been disseminated throughout her school. The tragic story quickly segued into one about the necessity of criminalizing the kids who dispersed the photo and about holding the schools accountable. In a *Today* show interview with Jesse's mother and the Internet expert Parry Aftab, Aftab noted that we need to enforce these laws "in order to keep our children alive."[4]

Hope Witsell, a thirteen-year-old in Florida, killed herself after a topless photo of her was sent around her high school and the high school in a neighboring town. She sent the photo after pressure to do so from a boy she had a crush on.[5] Really, though, the harm didn't originate with the sexting, which is how Witsell's and

Logan's cases were presented. It came from the girls' peers, who bullied them. The photos were just tools of a much greater harm, which is rarely addressed as seriously: slut shaming.

In January 2009, six teenagers faced child pornography charges for taking photos of themselves and being in possession of the photos. Three fourteen- and fifteen-year-old girls from their high school in Pennsylvania had sent seminude photos to the three sixteen- and seventeen-year-old boys. School officials seized the phones and reported them to the police, leading to the charges.[6] In Florida, a sixteen-year-old girl and her seventeen-year-old boyfriend, Phillip Albert, were charged with possession of child pornography. Albert, who is now twenty, sent a nude photo of his ex-girlfriend to seventy people out of anger after a fight with her. He was sentenced with child pornography charges and required to go on the public sex offender's list. He was kicked out of school, he struggles to find a job, and he can't even live with his father because his father lives near a high school, something Phillip is no longer allowed to do.[7]

But is sexting really worthy of such extreme policing? There has been much hesitating and changing minds in the courts, which suggests that we might be overreacting, typical of people's fears surrounding teenagers and sex.

Let's take a look at the data. In the 2008 study "Enhancing Child Safety & Online Technologies," by Harvard's Berkman Center for Internet and Society, researchers found that risky behavior online was generally in cahoots with risky behavior offline. Those who engaged in sexual acts away from their phones and the Internet tended to do so on their phones and the Internet as well. Indeed, almost half of sexually active teens tend to be involved in sexting and cyber-sex as well.[8]

Turned around, though, the statistics change. Sexting and sexual Internet activity does not seem to lead to real-life sexual activity among those who don't already engage in it. Regardless of all the increased access to sex online, teen sex rates haven't skyrocketed. In fact, they've lowered some during the past decade.

In my mind, we are missing the point regarding *what* to panic about. The issue isn't the "dicey mix of teenagers' age-old sexual curiosity, notoriously bad judgment and modern love of electronic sharing," as Riva Richmond called it in a *New York Times* article.[9] One could argue, in fact, that sexting is not only safe but also keeps kids safer than if they were having real-life sex.

No, the issue is that many girls—you guessed it, loose girls—use sexting and cybersex to try to feel wanted, and just like when they use male attention and sex in similar ways in real life, they don't get what they're after. When I asked the girls I interviewed why they sexted, their answers all pointed to a desire for connection. Amelia said, "It makes what is basically impossible to me possible, which is a hot guy liking me and wanting me in all ways."

"All ways?" I asked.

"Well, sexually, I guess," she said.

Amelia uses sexting and cybersex to pick up boys she likes who she meets in school or online, but is too shy to speak to in person. She contacts them and is immediately flirtatious. Within one or two exchanges, she starts in on the dirty talk. She engages in this way with them obsessively, and if they stop responding, or reject her in any way, she feels crushed.

Mariah has regularly had cybersex since she was in the eighth grade. When she discovered sexting, she started doing that regularly, too. Like the majority of females who report having sexted, she initially felt pressured to do so by the boys with whom she was texting. Over time, though, she grew to like the easy attention. Sexting and cybersex have pretty straightforward scripts, too, which only made it easier for her.

In real life, Mariah is still a virgin. She says she doesn't act the same way in person as she does via text and Internet, so boys don't realize the things she knows about sex. I asked Mariah what she felt she knew about sex, and she said, "Just that boys like it when girls act like sluts." Mariah doesn't connect her sexting and cybersex behavior with her own sexual arousal: the two hold completely different purposes. One is to get male attention, and the other is something private and personal, unrelated to how she might act under a boy's watch.

The danger here is not necessarily that girls are victims of predatory males. It's that they are victims of very narrow definitions of sexual desirability, and in many ways, sexting is one more way girls wind up viewing sexual behavior as completely removed from their own desires. Girls believe that a girl's desirability comes not from her personality or her coolness or how fun she is. It comes from her ability to fit into a male-defined stereotype of a sexually willing girl.

A recent national survey by the Girl Scouts Research Institute found that girls age 14–17 tend to describe themselves on social media sites as "fun," "funny," and "social," and they downplay the idea that they might be smart or ambitious, or otherwise less appealing to boys and popular cliques.[10]

Pornography sets a similar standard. Readers may be surprised to hear that lots of adolescent girls watch porn. There are no reliable statistics for this, of course, because girls are hard-pressed to admit it, but anecdotally, in my work and interviews with women and girls, about half have admitted to watching porn, some of them even watching regularly, as teens.

As with sexting and cybersex, there is no solid scientific evidence that exposure to pornography leads to widespread or predictable negative psychological effects, so again, we need to be careful where we put our energy regarding concerns about such exposure. In my experience working with teenage girls, they watched pornography partially because it turned them on and was an exciting avenue for masturbation, and partially because they wanted to know how to have sex.

The problem here is that girls think they are learning about sex, but really they're learning what men want. Shaved vaginas, asses in the air, facials—these are all male fantasies, not sex defined by females. Like Mariah noted, boys like girls who act like sluts. Porn just reinforces that. As Judith Levine writes, "In my opinion, the problem with sexual information on the Net is not that there is too much of it but that too little of it is any good"—and she wrote that in 2002.[11]

Almost a decade later, we can say that's changed some. There are a number of excellent websites intended to provide real information about real sex to teenagers (see the appendix for a list of these), sites that give teenagers answers to real concerns, and that don't exist for titillation.

And, then, there are the social sites—Facebook being the most influential. This is where hundreds of thousands of girls post pictures of themselves in bikinis or underwear to get attention from men. One guy wrote on the website *Facebook Horror Stories*, "Dear cute girls of Facebook, thank you for posting almost naked pictures of yourselves. I no longer need to look at porn since I have hundreds of photos of you in bikinis to whack off to. Thank you for inserting yourself into my spank bank."[12] This guy has caught on to the wave of loose girls looking for attention. Facebook has become an easy way for a loose girl to act out.

Cate has a bunch of photos of herself in her underwear in her album on Facebook. Every time she posts a new one, she told me, at least a couple guys who have been out of touch contact her again. It makes her feel good to know people think of her. I asked her what she thinks they contact her for. "I think that's pretty obvious," she said. "They just want to have sex with me. But it still makes me feel good."

"Good, as in worthwhile?" I asked.

"Exactly," she said.

Jennifer sends certain Facebook friends seminude photos when she feels like she's lost their attention.

"It works like a charm," she told me.

There are some real concerns about older men soliciting teenage girls via Facebook. A few cases have been reported, such as one about a thirty-four-year-old man in North Carolina who had a sexual relationship with a minor after getting to know her on Facebook, or the twenty-seven-year-old Pennsylvania man who changed his relationship status to "Engaged" to a fourteen-year-old girl (the joke in all the headlines was that there was no "statutory rape" relationship option).[13]

But while these men are clearly predatory, simply posting sexy photos to Facebook isn't necessarily dangerous, at least not in that way. Just like with sexting, the harm is mostly related to what the poster is hoping to get from having those photos up, and then what she actually gets. She gets attention for her body, of course. But what does that attention really mean about her? Of course, it means nothing. Having a nice body—or even just having a female body, which is all a girl really needs to get some male attention—doesn't take a girl very far in life.

Studies have made clear that most of what teenagers do on the Web can be considered positive. Most have a "full-time intimate community" they communicate with online—whether through instant messaging, Facebook, MySpace, or other sites—and they don't do much more than that. When they do, they seek information or experiment with digital media production, such as figuring out how to accomplish something on their own. A study done by the MacArthur Foundation determined that, although it may look like kids are wasting their time online, they are actually building technological skills and literacy, something needed to succeed in our modern world.[14]

Researchers have also found that Internet and cell phone communication leads to greater self-disclosure, which builds closer, more intimate relationships with friends.[15] This is another reason that websites providing real, frank information about sex—and an opportunity for questions—are so valuable. Where talking to parents is important, such a conversation can be embarrassing, for both parties. Even the most self-assured parents would be fooling themselves if they thought their teens were telling and asking them everything. We can think of resources online, and the self-disclosing conversations among peers, as bolsters to the support and education parents and schools can provide.

Parents will get nowhere, however, if their fears turn into what teenagers perceive as violations of privacy. Blocking their Internet usage, checking up on their computers, and wrangling passwords from their teens will only lead teenagers to tell even less, and the more open the lines of communication are between teenagers and adults concerning sex-related issues, the better.

Meanwhile, Johanna continues to send dirty texts, but she won't send any more photos. She told me that at some point she realized it was degrading.

"More degrading than the words?" I emailed.

"Yeah." She emailed back from her phone.

I asked her what she thought about other girls sending photos. "If a girl wants to do it, that's up to her," she said.

Her signature from the phone quoted her favorite band, Escape the Fate. "My heart's on an auction."

When I asked her what that meant to her, she said, "It sums me up."

PART TWO

GAINING POWER

Chapter 9

GROWN-UP GIRL

The Adult Loose Girl

*The loose girl is still in there. Sometimes in my dreams.
Sometimes in my fantasies. Sometimes in catching the eye of
the hot guy in line at the grocery store. I'm fifty-one years old
and have been a recovering loose girl since I was thirty-four.*

Laurie has been married for eighteen years now. She is in her fif-
ties, with two teenage boys. She and her husband make a good
living. They have a beautiful house in a great neighborhood,
two cars, and annual travel to other countries. She buys herself a
new wardrobe every year, and on each anniversary, her husband
buys her a new piece of jewelry. By anyone's standards, she is living
the good life. But if you look more closely, you will find a woman
who feels like she's still seventeen. She dresses every morning with
the thought of getting male attention. She works out, not for her
health, but so that a man might still find her attractive. She wor-
ries about getting older, about wrinkles and sagging. She goes to
a doctor to get some things done here and there—a little tuck or

plumping or whitening—all with the thought that she wants men to want her. Her husband doesn't know this, but she's always looking for men—when she is at the grocery store, at the bank, getting lunch when she's at work. She's always got her eyes open for the possibility of men.

There is, in fact, one man she works with. It was inevitable, she guesses. They flirt heavily, and she thinks about him as she puts on her clothes in the morning, wondering what he'll think. They smile from across the room. Something is going to happen. She knows it will. More, she wants it to. She doesn't know why. She loves her husband. They have no more problems than any other married couple. For the most part, their relationship is great. But this craving she has—she can't control it. She wants something to happen with the man at work. It's all she thinks about.

Laurie's story is like that of many other women who come to me. While we are worrying about our teen girls and their desperation around boys and sex, the women who used to be those girls are still there, too—grown-up loose girls, carrying the same pain, looking to get men's attention instead of boys'. One woman wrote me and asked, "What happens to old sluts?" It's an important question, one I intend to explore in this chapter.

A common goal for most women—and men, but more so women—is to get married. The marriage aspiration is reflected throughout our culture. In plenty of popular songs, such as Beyoncé's "All the Single Ladies" in which she sings, "If you liked it then you should've put a ring on it," pointing to her finger. Marriage is portrayed as what a girl deserves. If you want to be with me, in other words, you will need to marry me, because that's what I deserve. Many Hollywood movies and television series end with the engagement ring. It is the finale, the greatest possible attainment, the thing every girl should want above all else. Marriage means that you are chosen and wanted by someone, which is a loose girl's greatest desire.

I ended *Loose Girl* with my marriage, too, but I made a point of not closing the book that way. Instead, I showed a scene of myself in a bar, catching the eye of yet another boy. I didn't do anything more than look that evening, but I wanted to make clear to my readers that just because I was married didn't mean my struggle was over. I still spent too much time thinking about male attention. I still could easily let any situation where I felt wanted turn into another loose-girl event. The reaction to my ending was mixed. Bloggers wrote things like, "It seems to me she hasn't changed at all." Others liked the ambiguity. They felt this was more honest than suggesting I was all fixed by the end. Plenty interpreted the end to mean that they, too, could have real love some day, that they'd reach the "end" of something, which is a problem, I guess, with having to have an ending to the book. And plenty were irritated by the fact that I ended with a marriage. They wanted to see me changed in a way that didn't have anything to do with boys or men.

I stick to my intentions about ending that way because I wanted to emphasize that many loose girls marry like I did, and yet it doesn't mean anything, not really, about how we change. In many ways, I married to simply take myself out of the market. It's not that the man I'd met was magical, that he somehow knew how to love me in a way others couldn't. He was a good man, but he was still human with all the imperfections and difficulties that come along with that.

He did not save me from myself. He didn't transform me into some-one else. I was still me: the loose girl. The work of having intimacy had only just begun.

Being a loose girl is a lifelong process. I will always have to watch myself carefully, and I will surely always struggle. I will always make mistakes here and there. Whenever life gets hard, whenever some-thing makes me feel insignificant or unloved, whenever I feel aban-doned in any way, I tend toward my old behavior. I start thinking about a guy. I start considering how a man might save me. I start to slip. The main difference now is that those thoughts don't have the same power over me. I don't believe the fantasy. I'm too aware of its lie and how I've hurt myself with it.

But many women are not in the same place. They still struggle heavily with those feelings, still believe the pull, and still enjoy the high just a little too much.

Sandra has been having an affair for seven months now. She also sometimes sleeps with other men. Her husband probably knows, but he turns a blind eye. His anger comes out with passive aggres-sion and occasional verbal abuse. He tells her that she does things wrong or that she's too slow or too fast. He has pretty much stopped having sex with her, too. She knows her marriage needs to end, but she's scared that when she's on her own, her behavior will only get worse, that she'll feel out of control and will harm herself further.

This out-of-control feeling is typical among adult loose girls. They are ashamed that, at this point in their lives, when they should be making mature choices, they still act in these ways. But it feels like they can't stop. Often, as adults loose girls will fall into love and/or sex addiction. They tend toward unavailable men who will distance themselves as the women approach and pursue. Loose girls often demand too much too soon. They want to know if the men are going to commit to them pronto. They want to know how the men are going to make them feel loved. They expect men to fill their emptiness, and in adulthood, the loose girls feel angry that they don't. They call or email or text men too much, no longer feeling they have the luxury to wait. The pressure from society to settle down and marry is so immense that if a woman is single she often feels she is undesirable.

Or they remove themselves from men altogether. Gerri, who has been divorced for many years, told me that she hadn't been with a man in two years. She's been with more than a hundred men, and she just wants it to stop. She assumes she can't have a normal relationship with a man, so she won't go near any. She'd rather be alone than feel that out-of-control feeling that comes with her engagement with men.

The shame for grown-up loose girls is as bad as it is for teenagers, but it happens for an entirely different reason. Women should be married and monogamous (and heterosexual, for that matter). They should be concerned with their children, not with their own needs. They can have sex, unlike teenage girls, but they can't want it. And they certainly can't want it as much as or more than their partners. The stereotype of the married woman is that she is always warding off her husband's advances. There is that old caricature of the wife who says, "Not tonight, dear. I have a headache," and the underlying assumption that this is just an excuse for not wanting sex at all. There is that stereotype, too, of women sitting around together, complaining about their husbands' wanting sex. The notion is found on sitcoms, where the horny husband is always trying to get his wife to have more sex. Women fulfill their "wifely duty" by having sex, as though it is just one more thing they have to do, along with filling the dishwasher and cleaning the toilets.

Because of this stereotype, women often opt to not be sexual. It is much easier to be a married woman who doesn't desire sex. So, when you do desire sex, the shame and sense of being different, false as it is, can be a part of what keeps you in that loose-girl cycle, where you act out, feel ashamed, and then act out to try to feel better again.

Vivian, who is in her late thirties and has never married, fears her loose-girl behavior will keep her from ever finding a real relationship. She doesn't think she wants children, but she does feel like a relationship would make her feel worthwhile. She looks around and feels as though everyone else knows how to have this, that there must be something terribly wrong with her, and—her greatest fear—that she is in fact unlovable. She has had a number of long-term relationships where the man she is with eventually distances himself from her because, she claims, she gets too needy. When I asked her what she meant by "needy," she said she always wants more from him than he can give. She's so desperate for any man to choose her, to prove to her that she's worth loving, that she has no sense of wanting anything more specific from a man. In other words, she feels like she has no standards. Her only standard is that a man could love her and not leave. Tied up with this feeling is that she feels like she will sleep with anyone who will take her, in the hope that he will wind up loving her. I asked her if she actually wanted the sex itself. It took a while for her to answer: "I do want the sex," she said. "But it's not a straight answer, because I don't even know how to feel sexual desire without also needing something more. So, yes, I want the sex. But it's just because I want to feel close to a man." I asked her what happened in most cases. "In most cases, they don't stick around because I'm too needy. No one wants a needy girl."

Vivian's experience of sexual desire is similar to many teen girls' experience. She can't quite name her desire as pure sexual need. It's too interwoven with other needs, and as a result, the shame she feels is not just for wanting sex but for wanting anything. Her want becomes "neediness," because a wanting woman is unattractive. And Vivian notes that no one wants a "needy girl," reinforcing the idea that neediness belongs to girls, not women. The grown-up loose girl is so much like the teenage version that it is nearly impossible to tell them apart.

As discussed in chapter 3, slut pride can also get in the way for loose girls. Strong women should be able to sleep around, but for so many women, the sense that they aren't really strong, that they are in fact too needy, too ugly, too undesirable or unlovable, can get in the way. The slut-pride attitude gives women an avenue to act out their loose-girl behavior, which only makes them feel worse.

Many of them agree with the men who say they don't want to get serious; they just want to have sex and nothing more. But they're not telling the truth. When they reveal that they want more, and the men pull away, their neediness rises up, leading them to a further sense of shame (remember that a loose girl's greatest shame is not the fact that she has a lot of sex; it's that she feels as though her neediness makes her unlovable.) Grown-up loose girls struggle with the option of casual sex. They may want such a thing. They may, for instance, want sex but not a boyfriend after a marriage dissolves, but their constant need for male attention to translate into proof that they're lovable and worthwhile gets in the way. In this way, loose girls wind up damned if they do and damned if they don't.

Most loose girls claim that they want a close, intimate relationship with a man, but they feel incapable of having one, either because they can't get one or because once they do, they screw it up by needing too much and/or cheating. This is a big irony that loose girls face: many claim that all they want is a relationship, one in which they are truly loved by a man. But many times loose girls grow restless after they've gotten that, and they wind up looking outside the committed relationship for something new. When their emptiness, their sense of being worthless, isn't healed through the relationship, they head back out there, certain that it means they just didn't find the right one yet. Many women who come to me note that they don't understand why they do this, that they feel out of control, as though controlled by puppet strings, held by someone else. Indeed, they are being controlled by the addiction, by the pursuit of that high that comes when they feel like maybe this time they will get what they need to seal that void inside.

One of the biggest challenges grown-up loose girls face is recognizing that they have not lived in a vacuum. Like any other human, they have made mistakes. They learned negative patterns. They got themselves entangled in situations that they will never be free of. They have kids with the wrong people. They mess up their careers. The longer we live, after all, the more opportunities we have to love and lose. This is just a fact of life.

The media sets us all up to believe that somehow everyone else has perfect lives, everyone else gets their needs met all the time, but not us. Certainly, loose girls are guilty of this feeling. They assume that they are the only ones who can't get loved. They are the only ones obsessed with men. They are the only ones who mess up all their relationships. In truth, of course, most of us are like that. Life is suffering. Happiness is fleeting. So, the key to being a grown-up loose girl is acceptance. We will always struggle with these feelings. We will always think first of which guy can make us feel better. And we will always wrestle with neediness when the person we love goes away. The next chapter explores this idea of acceptance in much greater detail.

For most of my life I wanted to be "mysterious." This was one of my greatest aspirations. I just knew that if I were unreadable, if I were so taken up with my career or children or anything other than boys, if my needs weren't telegraphed to other people, that boys and men would pursue me constantly and I'd never feel unloved again.

I had plenty of reason to believe this. Our culture is very support-ive of what can be called "the rules girl," coined by Ellen Fein's and Sherrie Schneider's *The Rules* books, meant to capture Mr. Right.[1] A rules girl never calls a man back and never lets him know how interested she might be. She never looks nervous or uncertain. She needs nothing from men, and the second he stops fawning all over her, she goes away without shedding a tear (God forbid, or it might mess up her perfectly applied makeup).

The rules girl is, in other terms, the opposite of the loose girl. She is not needy, and she most certainly isn't slutty. And, of course, men adore her. A perfect example of this can be found on the reality show *The Hills*. Kristin Cavallari gets whatever guy she wants. She's beautiful and skinny, sure. So is Audrina, yet Justin Bobby keeps her at arm's length for years. But when Kristin enters his life, he's ready to commit. The same thing happened to Lauren Conrad back when *The Hills* was *Laguna Beach*. Lauren was in love with Stephen, who seemed to only have eyes for Kristin, even though everyone could see Kristin would break his heart and Lauren wouldn't. What did Kristin have that Audrina and Lauren didn't? She had the power that comes to a girl who doesn't give a flying you-know-what about whether that boy lives or dies. That's what she had.

The rules girl is held up in our culture as the girl you want—or want to be. In the books *Why Men Love Bitches* and *Why Men Marry Bitches*, the author Sherry Argov notes that men don't want the nice girl. They want the one who doesn't really have time for them. In *Make Every Man Want You* and the hundreds of titles along the same lines, the answer is all the same: they want the girl who is so caught up in her own life she could take or leave a guy. Recently, on *Jersey Shore*, Vinny fell hard for a girl because she stood him up. In Hollywood, the girl who isn't impressed by the leading male, the one who can't be bothered by him, is the one who wins him in the end. We loose girls—grown up now—get that message again and again: You still haven't figured out how to be the kind of girl who gets loved.

To this day, when I feel particularly unlovable I go back to the wish that I could be something other than I am. Really, we all have those things we wish we could change, don't we? There are some things we will be able to change and others we won't, as the well-known serenity prayer reminds us. We have to come to terms with those things that are core parts of our personality because they aren't changeable. It is good to acknowledge this. It is good for me to acknowledge, for instance, that I am never really distant, but that all men who would be with me will go through times of being a little distant. I can give men the space to love me, but I will be able to give only so much space. I share much about who I am. I don't do well keeping my feelings silent and unattended to. When I think I'm not getting enough attention, I ask what's going on. And so I will never be a rules girl, not without entirely denying who I am. And I'd rather like who I am than try to be someone else.

We know now that we live in a culture that has limited ideas about what we can be—men and women. Such a mind-set entirely belies the fact that humans are incredibly diverse. Add to this that many of us have been damaged along the way. We also live in a culture that has limited approaches to what love can look like: A man falls in love with a woman—usually a rules girl!—who also falls in love with him. Their every wish is fulfilled. Often they get married. And they live happily for the rest of their lives. Every romantic comedy, every Hollywood love story—*The Notebook*, *Titanic*, *My Best Friend's Wedding*, and *There's Something about Mary* are all popular examples—has this basic message inside it. Likewise, on television there is sitcom after sitcom in which the family is made up of husband and wife, and if it isn't, then that is the reason the sitcom exists because *how strange*! Every love song on the radio, every advertisement to get you to buy something: it is all to make us desire the same thing—being in healthy love with the same person forever.

In truth, half of our marriages end in divorce. People have affairs—60 percent of men and 40 percent of women (but 70 percent of married women and 54 percent of married men did not know of their spouses' extramarital activity).[2] We have blended families. We have open marriages. We have polyamory. We also have miserable marriages, loveless ones, sexless ones, deeply passionate and jealous and abusive ones. There are many, many ways to have love.

Recognizing this fact can be helpful for adult loose girls. It allows them the possibility of reenvisioning not just what they want, but what they can do right now. Perhaps they will be able to have this mainstream vision of love—if that's what they even want—but for now they can only have this other thing. If women give themselves the freedom to think outside the lines about what love can look like for them, they will be able to find some satisfaction.

Sami considers herself a loose girl. She spent most of her adolescence sleeping her way through her high school and the local bars, and in college she did more of the same. She did it because she was looking for someone to stay with her, but few of them did. In her twenties, she finally met someone who seemed to love her. Eventually they married, and Sami assumed that her life was complete. She had what she wanted. But as the years passed, she found herself anxious and unhappy. She sought counseling, which helped sometimes, but other times she just felt like wallowing in pointless pain. Her husband, frustrated with her unavailability, had an affair, and their marriage fell apart. For years afterward, Sami berated herself for how she ruined her marriage. She had everything she said she had ever wanted, and then she destroyed it all. She started another relationship, but about a year into it, she got those same edgy, anxious feelings. She felt miserable again. She went back into counseling again, but it only helped so much. Increasingly unhappy, she and her boyfriend broke up.

About five years later, she met another man and fell in love, but he lived in Europe, and she didn't want to disrupt her career. She fretted for months, and then she realized she didn't have to live with him. The more she thought about it, the more she realized she didn't want to. Her family was furious. Her friends told her she obviously had intimacy issues, but she was happy living so far from him. Their relationship worked like this. Her friends were right: she did have intimacy issues. Terrible ones. But what could she do about it? It was who she was. And the more she tried to be someone else, the worse she felt. She had figured out a way to be happy in a relationship, unconventional as it was.

It is possible that over time Sami will grow out of this stage of her life or will become capable of a different kind of intimacy, if that's her hope. But for now, she should be able to have love on her terms. What I'm really talking about here is humility. One of the greatest keys to emotional and psychological growth is humility. When we can look at ourselves honestly and without judgment, and can accept that this is our reflection, only then can there be the possibility of any change. People don't like this. They tell me, "You mustn't give up," which is not at all how I see it. They say that I will have real love if I hand over my life to Jesus or if I try their newfangled therapy.

But acceptance *is* real love. There is no greater love. It provides more intimacy with oneself than anything else. The longer adult loose girls spend trying to be something else, trying to change themselves into something they aren't, the longer they will feel ashamed of who they are. Meanwhile, loose girls can have love, too. It just may not look like it does for everyone else—at least not at first. If the old adage that you can't be in love until you love yourself first is true, then loose girls have to learn to love themselves for not loving themselves. It is the first rule of acceptance, which is also the first step toward real intimacy for loose girls.

Chapter 10

THE BEGINNING OF CHANGE

I'm still here, I move around to try to get a new me,
but I still remain the same. And now I'm moving
again, this time with a real hope to make it work,
to change things, to rip off this part of me.

When my husband and I got engaged, I threw myself into wedding planning. I needed to believe that my life was about to change—not just that I would be a wife, settled down, but that I would somehow stop feeling that old desperation that had continually gotten me into trouble with men. I figured that by taking my game piece off the table, that part of me would evaporate. Someone loved me. He loved me enough to marry me. What's more, he was wonderful—kind, attentive, *available*. I no longer needed to spend my time searching for what I didn't quite get yet was pure fantasy. I no longer needed to try to fill my emptiness. It would be filled now through my marriage.

A few months after the wedding, though, I found myself out again at a bar. There was a guy there. Beautiful—big eyes and full lips. He brushed his hair back from his face with his hand. He turned his eyes to me, and it was as though the entire world went away. There was no husband, no marriage. No friends at my table. No noise. There was me and there was this guy, a guy who would surely penetrate my pain, who would show me through his attention to me that I was worthwhile.

Later that night, having left alone, dodging that boy's advances, I sat in the bedroom where my husband unknowingly slept and tried to calm myself. In truth, I was terrified. Would I ever be free of the grip of my addiction? Would I be able to stay committed to this man I loved, who loved me? That evening I understood in a deeper manner that I would always be that girl. Marriage would not release me from her. Being loved by a man would not shake her loose. She and I were one. I would need to consider how to live my life with her.

That night was an important turning point for me as a loose girl. It was the beginning of my movement toward true intimacy— perhaps not intimacy as our culture defines it, where a man and a woman fall in love and ride off into the sunset and all is forever right with the world—but *movement* toward intimacy, which is the greatest achievement for a loose girl.

Perhaps you have a daughter who you want to protect. Perhaps she has already begun heading down this path. Perhaps you are a therapist who regularly hears stories just like these from your clients. Or maybe you are the girl you see in these pages. You are the one seeking change. This chapter is indeed about change. Readers write me daily: "Tell me what to do. Tell me how to change." To talk about change for a loose girl, we must first talk about not changing, because the bottom line is that it remains highly unlikely that you will stop feeling that urge to seek male attention when you are feeling low. As noted in the previous chapter, and like with any addiction, the first step is acceptance. Here, we examine the idea of acceptance more closely.

LOVING YOURSELF

Most of the women who spoke to me have been told at one time or another that they must love themselves before someone else will love them. Friends tell them. Therapists tell them. Their parents tell them, too. For a loose girl, though, it isn't that simple. For most of us, loving ourselves is too complicated. We've screwed up too many times. We've pushed too many people away with our addictions. We've gotten pregnant, had abortions, put ourselves in situations where we were mistreated again and again. We are too miserable when we're alone. Other people can love themselves first, but not us. When I asked a few of the women what they thought of when they heard "love yourself," they grew silent. Mandy said she'd never really thought about what that would even entail. Carla said she guessed she was supposed to take spa days, or lavender baths, or have a candlelit dinner for one. We laughed, hearing how ridiculous that was.

Loving yourself is a lifelong process of acceptance for who you are. It is a process of acknowledging the ways you've screwed up, harmed yourself, done irreparable damage to relationships, and still seeing that you are a worthwhile human being. You won't get there by taking a bath. Loving yourself is part of an endless movement toward intimacy. The women I interviewed who felt they were more in control of their loose girl than in the past all said something similar about accepting themselves as they were.

"You have to learn to be happy with who you are and the way God created you."
   "I don't think anyone ever recovers from this, only manages."
   "I consider myself in the process of heading towards recovery."
   "I still have a difficult time being vulnerable and intimate but at least I am aware of it."

Before we can have intimacy with anyone else, we must find a way to accept ourselves. But girls who have sex are not treated kindly in American culture. You are a slut. You don't care about yourself. You don't care about having real love. Otherwise, you wouldn't stand before the mirror before you go out, trying to determine which skirt best shows off your legs. Or, if you aren't a slut, you are the empowered girl discussed in chapter 3; you have sex because, by God, you can do whatever you want to do. You can go out in the evening and collect boys like fireflies in a jar. You don't have to want love.

All these assumptions made about you sink into your sense of self. It is nearly impossible to keep out the voices of a culture that will not let girls define their sexual identity. And then, too, there are parents and friends and ex-boyfriends and boys at school— all of them make assumptions about who we are as sexual beings. Inevitably, we feel judged, defensive, hurt, and misunderstood.

So, before you can begin to have intimacy with yourself and others, before you can make choices for yourself that aren't self-destructive, you must first embrace the part of you that needs. This is a hard one. Just hearing that feels wrong. Girls aren't supposed to need. Our neediness is ugly. It pushes boys away. It's the reason we are unlovable. These are the lies we believe—that girls should not crave anything. We shouldn't have intense desires. Open any book called *How to Make a Man Love You* or some version of that title, and the number one rule is don't be needy. Boys *hate* that, they all say.

Mandy, twenty-three years old, explains that her neediness feels like "an open sore." She says, "Every time I start to like a boy it's like I can't control myself. I can't act cool anymore. I call too much. I say too much. I know I make myself unattractive, and I hate it. Sometimes I wish I could just rip my neediness out of my body." Mandy isn't alone with this feeling. I hear this sense of repulsion regularly from girls when they talk about their neediness. I felt that way, too. The shame I had from my need in my teens and twenties was so intense, in fact, that it threw me back into yet another boy's bed again and again. Shame about one's need is one of the defining features of the loose girl.

However, when a girl acts needy with a boy, if she, like Mandy says, calls him again and again and he doesn't call her back, leaves messages saying, "Why haven't you called? Don't you like me anymore?" then what she is really doing is trying to control him with her need. We girls do all sorts of things like this, don't we? Some of us send too many emails and texts. Some hang on him in public, afraid he'll look at someone else. Some break into his Facebook account to see if he's talking with other girls. This kind of behavior among girls is almost considered normal.

A few weeks ago at a nail salon, I heard a woman breezily say to her friend, "I figured he was cheating on me again, so I broke into his email account to see if I was crazy." (Honey, once you've broken into his email account, there's nothing more to see about whether you've crossed over into crazy.) "*Women*," the guys all say, rolling their eyes. And sure enough, girls call each other to talk about these actions, to get support for them. "Of course you had to break into his account! He was acting weird!" "Of course you called him again! He still hasn't called you back! What does he expect you to do?"

But this isn't normal behavior. When we engage in these sorts of behaviors, we have moved so far away from ourselves, from caring about ourselves, from being a friend to ourselves, that we are so completely out of control that we may as well be drinking until we puke or shooting our arms full of drugs. When a girl relentlessly pursues a guy to find out what he's thinking, she is demanding that he make her feel better, that he feed a part of her that has nothing to do with him by calling her back and saying, "Of course I like you." When she breaks into his accounts, she is suggesting that he can't have a will of his own, that there is no way he would love her if she doesn't control him into doing so. Who in their right mind likes that? Who finds that attractive? Nobody wants to be made responsible for another person's feelings. You don't have to be a boy to feel that way. Girls don't want to have a boy's desperation dumped on them either. The problem here is not the neediness itself. It's making other people responsible for your needs. It's acting on no one's behalf, not even your own. It is acting without any compassion for him and his needs, or for you and your own.

Beneath all that chasing and pursuing and desperation, of course, there is a little girl, a girl who feels abandoned every time you don't give her attention and try to make someone else—a boy—take care of her. There is a little girl who doesn't believe for a moment that anyone would love her if she didn't try to force them into it. Some of the women I spoke with had had experiences in therapy where the therapist had tried to help them find this girl and take care of her. Twenty-seven-year-old Carla described how useless that was:

The therapist had me close my eyes and try to visualize the part of me that felt needy as a small child. I did it too. She was in there, like in my stomach, or maybe my womb. She was probably about six or seven. The therapist had me like kiss her and hug her and stuff, and even though I did it, the whole time I was thinking how ridiculous it was. I mean, I could love this part of me all I want, but as a woman I was still going to want a man to love me.

Carla's story exemplifies how many of the therapeutic approaches to help us *stop* needing male attention probably won't help. There are lots of exceptions, of course. Some women will find success with twelve-step programs or with the sort of visualization that Carla described. But most of us don't, because unlike most addictions, part of what we are after is perfectly healthy—love, attention, and sex. Not only is it perfectly healthy, but it's also necessary to a satisfying life.

So, before anything else, girls like us have to accept that that part of us that desperately wants attention, that desperately wants to be loved, is never going away. That time is past. Way back when, my mother didn't love me enough, caught up in her own narcissism. Mandy's father left when she was two years old, and she can count the amount of times she's seen him since on one hand. Carla's parents were so busy with their own unhappiness that they didn't care to see hers. The other girls and women I spoke to had mothers who tried to kill themselves, fathers who ignored them, fathers who bullied and were sexually inappropriate or outright molested. Others were raped or simply became caught up in the cultural pressure to be sexy and to put out so that guys would find them worthwhile.

We all have our stories. They are ours to keep, a part of what makes us who we are. We will never be rid of them. Never. When you can swallow that fact, when you can acknowledge that you will always feel that ache, that it will resurface every once in a while, and that it is only yours and that no one else has the capacity to make it feel better, then you are ready to move toward real change.

SHARING OUR STORIES

Leigh knows she will always be a loose girl, and in some ways, that was the truth that helped her feel like she could move forward with her life. She spent her teens and most of her twenties trying desperately to get male attention, trying to turn every glance from a man into a relationship. By the time she met Chris, the man she'd wind up marrying, she knew she had to find a way to stop relying so much on men to make her feel worthwhile. She came to me at that point, wanting to hear how she could not screw up her relationship with Chris. When I told her the first step was to acknowledge that she would always feel the way she feels, that she would always have the propensity to seek out other men, she grew angry. She said, "How does that help me?" But over time, she saw that it was true. To change her behavior, she had to stop beating herself up for her feelings. She had to recognize that she had those feelings again and again to know that she need not act on them. Just because she felt the desire didn't mean she had to act on it.

The other process that helped Leigh was finding a group of women who struggled like she did. Many psychologists understand that stories can heal. Sharing stories—telling your own and listening to those of others—is a therapeutic process. Much has been written about using narrative in psychotherapy—psychodynamic and cognitive-behavioral therapies—as a way to help clients integrate their histories, their multiple selves, and as a way to make better choices. When we tell our stories, we are forced both to claim ourselves ("I did this") and to claim our responsibilities to other people, such as our families and communities. When we tell our stories, and when our audience demands vulnerability from us, we can no longer get away with behavior like breaking into Facebook accounts. Suddenly, it is just us and our feelings and the question of what we will do with them.

I would argue that the group experience of knowing that you're not alone—particularly for issues such as promiscuity, where girls carry so much shame—is useful as well. So many of us have these stories, and yet so few feel safe sharing them. After *Loose Girl* came out, I set up a system on my website where girls could simply submit their loose girl stories and read others' in the hope that knowing so many of us are out there would be healing.

EXAMINING THE THINGS WE TELL OURSELVES

Any girl or woman I've worked with who is still in the throes of loose-girl behavior, still pursuing male attention at any cost, even as it makes her feel like garbage, believes in the fantasy she has about men. With each of these women I've asked the same question: "What do you believe he will do for you?" Their answers are almost all the same:

"He will love me the way no one ever has before."
"He will make me happy."
"He will save me."

A huge part of being a loose girl is believing in a fantasy, and that fantasy is of course not factual. We have been handed the lie about men by our media and culture. A boy will make you worth something. A boy's loving you means you matter in the world. We've bought the idea entirely. But beneath the fantasy is the blatant lie. It isn't true. Not even close. No man's attention to a girl means anything. In fact, more often than not it just means he has an opportunity to use her for sex, which, in the typical cultural irony for a girl, makes her matter less. Perhaps more important, whatever fantasy you or your daughter or your client or student carries around is based on some lack that can't possibly be filled by another person, and most certainly not some random boy. That emptiness is very real, but the fantasy that someone will fill it is not.

Often, when it comes into their awareness that they have these beliefs, the girls and women I work with are surprised. I encourage them to write those beliefs down on one side of a piece of paper, and then to make a list on the other side of what those men actually wind up doing for them. This is important, because even if men do provide some positives in these women's lives, they do not do this impossible task of filling their emptiness, of taking away or saving them from their pain.

Larissa believed that every boy that gave her attention, or who she developed a crush on, would be "the one." When I pressed her about what she meant by "the one," she admitted he would be the one who would love her so much that all her pain would go away and she'd always be happy. Larissa grew up with parents she described as "distant," whom she was never able to feel loved by. After she wrote down this belief, we discussed what she really did get from these boys. She determined that she got some affection and some sense that she was pretty and desirable, but little else. She said she never even felt like they were her friends. I didn't expect this to change everything for Larissa right away, but it was a task I suggested she repeat with each encounter or crush. The more she paid attention to her fantasy about boys, the easier time she would have unraveling why it felt so terrible when it didn't work out, and let's face it—it was never going to work out as long as those were her expectations.

Deb provides another example. She had a boyfriend, but she cheated on him constantly. When I asked her what she wanted from him, she told me that she wanted him to make her feel whole. These sorts of answers are so common. We hear them everywhere. They are spread across our media, in every teen drama and romantic comedy. *A boy will complete you.* It's yet another line delivered that rarely does any good for teen girls. Clearly, though, she didn't feel whole. She slept with other boys because she felt desperate and uncared for, and she secretly hoped one of these other boys would give her that sense of wholeness. Deb and I stayed in touch, and though she hadn't stopped searching for that sense of wholeness, she could see how she had reached that point and needed to make a change.

Along with the fantasy about boys are the core beliefs—called core schemas in cognitive therapy—we have about ourselves. So often, we come to believe some essential lie about ourselves: *I am not lovable. I am not special. I am worthless. I don't matter.* These lies come about through various channels, such as growing up with parental abuse or neglect or addiction, or with a trauma such as rape. Or they come about because of situations with boys, or because of our personality type, or simply because of how our culture makes us feel as girls.

Paula, for instance, developed the core belief "I am not special" right after she went through puberty. She developed crushes on boys, but those boys kept choosing other girls to date. When one finally did choose her as his girlfriend, he decided he liked someone else after about a month. This is ordinary dating behavior among adolescents, but Paula felt as though it meant she were different from other girls, that she wasn't special.

Combine those sorts of core beliefs with the fantasy of what a boy can provide, and it's easy to see why a girl might get hung up on getting with boys. She can easily come to believe that a boy will save her from these terrible things she believes about herself. He can make them untrue. I encouraged Paula to notice when she had that thought about not being special, and then we worked together to examine the thought process that led her to that false belief. Over time, she began to recognize that there was little logic to it. Having this sort of awareness so young—fourteen years old—Paula has the potential to avoid heading down a loose-girl path.

MAKING NEW HABITS

Deb was in the perfect mind space for changing her behavior, for creating new habits. One of the dangers of loose-girl self-harming sexual activity is that your brain develops habits. In the same way that one might develop a psychological dependence on a glass of wine in the evening, or a few hits of marijuana to sleep, girls (and boys) can develop a psychological dependence on promiscuity (as with other process addictions). Deb, for instance, knew she was making bad choices. She knew she had a false fantasy, and she hardly believed in it anymore. But just knowing is sometimes not enough. Often the behavior is entrenched enough that we have to *do* things differently, too.

It's important to note that often the predictable pattern feels good. Something about that drama and pain, something about getting to feel the feelings we usually tamp down, feels good. Think about any other sort of addictive pattern. Imagine you were a heroin addict. Imagine the ritualized process of calling your dealer, driving into that seedy part of town. The haggard people on the streets.

Your heart beats wildly in your chest. You know that you will get that feeling again. Then after doing that drug, imagine how it feels to come down and feel desperate for more, how familiar it is. The process is almost comforting, even as you start to sweat and feel sick. You know it by heart. This is the same for the loose girl. She gets pleasure from the process, even as it feels like hell. Those familiar neurons fire, those same sections of the brain light up, the various neurochemicals begin their work. The loose girl must acknowledge this buzz as part of her necessary awareness.

In most therapies for substance abuse, the addict is told to commit to staying away from his or her triggers, and that absolutely applies to the loose girl. If she usually messes around with boys at parties and regrets it later, she should stay away from parties. If she gives blow jobs in the school stairwell, she should stay away from the stairwell. Not forever. Just until new habits can take hold.

There are a number of established studies about how behavior changes, and they all point to the idea that there is a limited period of time in which a habit should change. The best documented is the work of Prochaska, Norcross, and DiClemente, who determined through research that habits form after just about twenty-one days. They also established the "stages of change" approach, which recognizes that people are in precontemplation, contemplation, or preparation, all before reaching action and maintenance; it's important to know where one is among these stages before trying to change.[1]

Thus far, I've been encouraging the contemplation stage, where you build awareness about your issue and begin to believe you might want change. Put another way, I've been encouraging readers to move out of precontemplation and into contemplation. Assessing what your triggers are, such as parties, is part of the preparation. When you are ready to commit, you can move out of preparation and into action, which I discuss shortly. Maintenance comes with the gradual rewards that arrive, although they don't arrive quickly. First, lots of challenges come, including the opportunity to relapse, which commonly happens and is no reason to give up. Finally, environmental controls are established, and often the person who changes does some sort of work in the world—perhaps as a therapist or writer or teacher—to help others with change, too.

Something I appreciate about the stages-of-change model is that it acknowledges that not everyone is ready to change. I would take this a step further and say that we should never judge where a person is. Not one of us knows what it's like to be anyone else, what resources a person has internally and externally. When you aren't ready to change something in your life, you aren't ready. That's all there is to it. You can try to force it. You can beat yourself up about it. But it will happen when it happens. The human psyche is not readable that way, and thank goodness. We are multifaceted and complicated, and that humanness is beautiful enough to keep me in love with my work. Be patient with yourself. Accept where you are.

This is a good place to note the myths about change, and in particular about change for a loose girl. The first myth is that change is simple. Of course, some have an easy time changing, but we hate those people (kidding!). Most don't have an easy time. Most, in fact, have tried many things. Change for a person who is deeply entrenched in a habit, who is acting addictively, is not easy.

A closely related myth is that willpower leads to change. Willpower is necessary, of course, to reach a place at which you will commit to change. But it is only a small piece of change. For a loose girl, she needs willpower to not go to that party where the boys are, especially when she's feeling down on herself. But the willpower isn't enough. She needs to engage in a circuit of efforts, including social support, acceptance of herself, and self-awareness about her fantasies. She needs to be willing to sit through some pretty painful feelings that come when she doesn't relieve her anxiety with male attention.

The other important myth here is the magic bullet. Our society can probably be blamed for much of the origins of the magic bullet. We do not cater to patience or discomfort. Technology has practically removed the word *slow* from our vocabulary. Everything is immediate gratification. Unfortunately—or fortunately, depending how you look at it—personal change won't ever be fast. If it is, then I guarantee you it isn't real. There is nothing—no pill you can take, no shot you can get, no new-age therapy you can do—that will take away your shame or your pain or your propensity to act out with boys. I often remind my clients—and myself—that this is a lifelong process. It is more than possible that you will never be fully free of it. Embrace that.

CREATING RULES

So, action. The first action is to remove your triggers. You can think of this like rules. Here are some examples:

"I may not go to the bar until further notice."

"I must remove Dylan's phone number from my phone and never contact him again."

"I may not text a boy back until he has texted me twice first."

Rules are terribly useful. You can write them on sticky notes or in your phone. Refer to them often. Pull them out whenever you need. Addicts in general, and loose girls in particular, need rules because we often live our lives out of control. In fact, loose-girl behavior can be a failed way to try to get control.

EMBRACING DISTRACTIONS

Along with rules, loose girls need a list of distractions they can turn to when necessary. Examples of distractions are exercise, calling a particular friend who won't judge you, chopping firewood, knitting, cooking, or playing piano. It seems simple, but it really is a necessary part of the process, because when a loose girl doesn't go out boy hunting or doesn't text the guy she knows will grant her a booty call and then ignore her afterward, even with all her awareness about her patterns, she will experience anxiety. And distractions will help her cope.

FEELING THE FEELINGS

Let's go back to Larissa's story. Every time Larissa reached out to a boy, she did so out of anxiety. Her anxiety about her pain, about her unhappiness, was the real trigger that led her to seek out another boy. Her anxiety rose up, and without thinking, she sought out the next guy to quell it. This anxiety is one of the greatest challenges. There's a reason girls keep pursuing what makes them feel like crap soon after. That reason, in a momentary sense, is anxiety. One thing we know about anxiety is that it is very treatable with behavioral methods. Anxiety is simply a resistance to feeling. It's fear of feeling. In that way, it is irrational fear. Anxiety generally won't kill you. So one of the best ways to treat anxiety is to extinguish the fear feelings that go along with it, and the way to do that is to simply *feel the feelings*. No doubt, anxiety is scary, but when you let yourself feel the terrible fear, when you feel that awful pain you've been avoiding for years, you find you live through it. You may be debilitated for a bit. You may have to stay in bed for a weekend and cry. You may have to yowl and scream. That is OK. You will still live through it. And you can tell yourself this all the way through: "This is just the pain I never let myself feel. It feels this bad because I've avoided it for so long. I'm going to come out the other side."

The next time, it won't be quite as bad, and the next time a little less. Over time, it may always be painful, but you'll feel it, you'll cry or whatever it is you do to move through it, and then you'll carry on. It is painful, just like the behavior with boys was painful, but at least this pain is in your control, and you aren't demanding anything from others in the process.

OTHER PROGRAMS

There are other approaches to treatment out there. Some loose girls have connected to the approach found in Sex and Love Addicts

Anonymous (SLAA), since there is plenty of overlap between the loose girl's experience and someone who identifies as a sex or love addict.[2] Others try alternative approaches, such as therapies that address posttraumatic stress disorder, or obsessive-compulsive disorder, or anxiety disorders in general. It is important to find what you respond to. The main thing to remember is that change is ongoing. Your pain will always be your pain. No one—really, *no one*—will save you. It is just a decision, and when you are ready, when your daughter is ready, when your client is ready, you, she, will do this.

At the end of a chapter about change for the loose girl, we must restate where the chapter started. You will always be this girl. You will never go through a struggle in life without finding yourself up against these thoughts or desires. You will not magically become someone new. Change is a journey, with no clear end point.

Chapter 11

WAVES

Protecting against Loose-Girl Behavior

J o is a single mother and former loose girl who has been doing her best to work though her own issues with male attention as she raises her teenage daughter. "I'm so worried," she told me, "that I won't be able to help her. I try to behave in ways that will show her a woman can make good choices. But sometimes it feels like a failed effort." When I asked her what she meant she spoke about all the magazines, the television shows, her daughter's friends, and the boys. "I feel helpless in a world that has already determined what will happen to my daughter. She'll think everything she needs comes from some guy, and she'll never believe in herself enough to be everything I know she can be." After a few moments, she added, "I don't mean that. I sound so pessimistic."

Beyond the loose girl, beyond the shame, the behavior, the question of right or wrong, beyond all the dirty little secrets, is the culture that created this dilemma for girls. In so many ways, Jo is right. Her daughter doesn't have a fighting chance against the cultural wave explored in chapter 1.

Parents ask me often, "How can I protect my girls?" Colleagues in psychology and education wonder, "Is it even possible to prevent what happens to girls regarding sex?" This chapter explores this idea of prevention, how we can work to overhaul the culture to do so.

When I asked Jo what she *is* doing, she said she's doing the opposite of what her parents did. Her parents told Jo not to have sex. That was it. Just don't do it. Jo recognizes that telling her daughter to stay away from boys, or to not have sex, would be useless. She said, "I don't want to do that to her. She should have sex! Oh God, I'm sure parents all over the world would judge me for that one. I think she should be able to have sex. I just don't want it to become her whole life, like it did for me."

For decades, the push has been along the same lines as what Jo's parents told her. And the results have been consistent: nothing has changed. The large majority of those who pledge abstinence at thirteen lose their virginities by sixteen and are just as likely to engage in oral and anal sex as those who didn't pledge, according to a study sponsored by the National Institutes of Health.[1] With limited guidance and plenty of shame about contraception, they wind up with STDs and pregnancies. They get married too young, to the wrong person, because they just want to have sex already and not be judged as bad. Many become what we can now define as loose girls, young women who use sex and male attention to fill emptiness and need, who wind up disappointed and ashamed, unsure how to change their behavior, and terribly judged.

Jocelyn M. Elders, in her foreword to Judith Levine's book *Harmful to Minors: The Perils of Protecting Children from Sex*, wrote:

We lead the Western world in virtually every sexual problem: teenage pregnancy, abortion, rape, incest, child abuse, sexually transmitted disease, HIV/AIDS, and many more. Yet when the Surgeon General issues a call to action on sexual health urging comprehensive sex education, abstinence, and other measures to promote responsible sexual behavior, and advocates that we break our "conspiracy of silence about sexuality," we want to fire the Surgeon General.[2]

We are caught in an odd rigidity on this issue, one that is burdened with false, fear-inducing dangers about what it is to be a girl, when meanwhile the biggest danger of being a girl is how impossible it is to wade through the fear-inducing propaganda to find the truth.

When the child psychologist G. Stanley Hall coined the term *adolescence*, sexuality came to be seen as more of a test than a natural progression. It became a danger to traverse, a danger that adolescents must not allow to take over their lives to avoid future problems, such as impulsivity. Like Freud's theories about sexual stages, this was simply another theory, certainly not evidenced by research. This isn't to say Hall's notion of adolescence hasn't been immensely useful. Obviously, it has. My comment is only to point out that our panic about girls having sex is based on a man-made philosophy, not empirically supported research, and is therefore worthy of questioning.

It is important to note these odd biases, because they are so hugely in the way of us making any headway on the very real cultural issues attached to girls and sexuality. We must begin to change our minds about how to transform the culture when it comes to teen girls and sex.

Jacquie went to school in the Midwest, among cornfields and wheat. Her experience of sex education involved anatomical drawings of the reproductive sex organs (but not the clitoris, she told me when I asked) and a whole lot of information about how to protect herself from boys. The boys were in another classroom, getting their own education. When I asked what the boys learned about, she said that she didn't know but suspected they weren't being taught to protect themselves from girls. She's right. Most sex education for boys is limited to anatomy, birth-control options, and wet dreams.

While she was being taught how to say no, she regularly wondered how to say yes. Was that even possible for a girl? She was itching to experiment. For one, she was horny, like any healthy adolescent girl. For another, she was curious. Incidentally, she told me, she gained nothing from her sex-ed curriculum and wound up pregnant at sixteen. She had an abortion, and her born-again Christian mother kicked her out of the house. She has been unable to have a healthy relationship with almost anyone since. She told me, "Sometimes I think I'm not cut out to love and be loved. Is that possible, that some people are just too fucked up to get loved?"

Jacquie is a strong—and awfully sad—example of how sex education fails girls. It sets up the same lie girls are sold everywhere: boys are horny; you are not. Boys get what they want; you get to be there for their purposes. So be careful. And always the underlying message is there for girls: don't act on your sexual urges or you will be immoral and unworthy. In essence, we set our kids up for failure when it comes to sex.

Clearly, the just-say-no approach doesn't work. When we continue to take this approach, we bang our heads against the wall of increasing teen pregnancy, STDs, and exceeding confusion and desperation about what sex means. Abstinence education fails girls. The statistics bear this fact out. There is no difference statistically between those who pledge abstinence and those who don't. In the 1990s, there was a slight drop in teen pregnancies and STDs, which, not surprisingly, abstinence advocates jumped all over as evidence that abstinence works. But both the Alan Guttmacher Institute and the Centers for Disease Control and Prevention determined through closer research that the drop was due to increased contraceptive use and increased engagement in sex other than vaginal intercourse.[3] Unprotected vaginal intercourse had declined, not intercourse and sex itself.

Judith Levine writes, "Abstinence education is not practical. It is ideological."[4] And still, we cling to it. This is likely because conservatives see teenagers having any sexual relations as the problem. But as we've explored in this book, the harm is not in the sex but in the circumstances in which sex can happen, such as girls having sex solely because they want to feel cared for, or girls having sex without protection because they want to please the boy more than they want to protect themselves.

Good sex—when a girl wants to have the sex, both physically and emotionally, and when she does what she needs to protect herself physically—cannot be a bad thing, and certainly not any worse than it is for a boy. We all know that teen boys and girls are sexually desirous creatures. They want sex! And they *will* have it. Holding fast to the idea that sex is bad for teens has no useful purpose except to harm teenagers by shaming them—particularly girls—when they do have sex.

In 2000, the National Campaign to Prevent Teen Pregnancy took a poll and found that almost three-quarters of girls who had had sex regretted it, where about half the boys did.[5] It shouldn't surprise us to learn that a spokesperson for the campaign said that the results showed that teens were taking a more cautious attitude toward sex. But if we look at the numbers through a different lens, we can see that the statistics translate more into shame than caution—and of course girls carry the larger burden of that shame. A handful of young women approached me after reading *Loose Girl* to say that they related because they had premarital sex and wished they hadn't, evidence that in too many girls' minds, any sex before marriage makes them disgraceful. I've asked a few of those girls why they thought that made them disgraceful, and they all answered that they shouldn't even have *wanted* to have had sex.

Missing from sex-education curricula is really anything that might help a teenager know what to do with her sexual feelings. Sure, she can identify the ovaries on the diagram, but she knows nothing about her desire, or a boy's desire, or how to protect herself physically and *emotionally* during sexual acts.

One listen to *Loveline*, the late-night call-in radio show with Dr. Drew Pinsky, reveals the intense lack of sexual self-knowledge among teens. And most of it is attached to shame. By example, three times in two weeks various girls called in to find out whether there was something wrong with them because their vaginas got very wet when they were excited. Dr. Drew had to reassure all of them that each person has different amounts of secretion when sexually aroused. Go to any of the teen sex Q&A websites and you'll see questions about whether anal sex can get you pregnant or about whether something is wrong when a girl orgasms just thinking about a sexual fantasy.

Included here are ideas for sex education that might truly help girls (and boys!) understand what sex is about, what is happening in their bodies, and how to make decisions about both.

TRUE SEX EDUCATION

1. Talk about Desire

How would *you* answer this question from your daughter: "How will I know when I'm ready to have sex?" The answer is, of course, individual to each girl, but very few mothers, educators, and therapists think to include some attention to a girl's sexual desire as part of their answer. The bottom line about girls and healthy sexuality is that this must be part of how we talk to girls about sex. Usually, we hand down to them the same useless, often harmful myths. We tell them that sex will get in the way of their happiness and growth. We tell them they must be in love. We tell them that good sex happens only when you are in love. None of those aphorisms is true—not one. Sex and sexual feelings are essential to our happiness. Sex does not make sense only when you are in love. And sex with someone you aren't in love with can be just as good as sex with someone you do love. Add desire—the acknowledgment that girls have sexual desire—into the answer, and everything can change. Everything becomes more—true.

For one, we can encourage girls to learn to trust their bodies and what their bodies tell them. We can also tell them that just because they want it sexually doesn't mean it will be worth it or any good. We can tell them that sex with someone who wants you to enjoy yourself is a hundred times better than sex with someone who doesn't care about your experience, and sex with someone you love *and* who cares about your experience might be even better.

2. Talk about Outercourse

Another assumption we make as a culture is that to fulfill sexual feelings, people must have intercourse. This is absolutely untrue. Sex therapists use the term *outercourse* to describe the numerous acts that create sensual and sexual pleasure but do not include penetration. Think hand jobs. Think second and third base. Think phone sex. For teens who are experiencing that hormone rush but aren't ready to expose themselves to possible pregnancies and STDs, outercourse is perfect.

More than that, outercourse allows a teenager to explore and test intimacy, which is essential for building the self-confidence girls need to be both powerful and self-protected in the world of relationships. One sex therapist notes that communication is enhanced during outercourse. Because the sexual sensations can be less intense, there is more opportunity for closeness, for talking, and for full consent from both parties. And, let's face it, the likelihood of a girl having an orgasm via outercourse is much better than during intercourse. Boys benefit too. Boys receive plenty of cultural pressure to have as much sex as they can, even when they aren't ready to do so emotionally, so outercourse is a more gentle introduction into the world of sexual feelings and intimacy. In case I need to clarify, I believe it makes sense to include outercourse in sex education.

3. Talk about Masturbation

It also makes sense to include masturbation in a sex-education curriculum as a healthy, satisfying way to fulfill sexual desire, especially since a greater proportion of girls between fourteen and seventeen years old report solo masturbation than any other sexual activity. Adolescents have sexual desire. More so, they are in the process of learning about their sexual desire. What better way for adolescents to learn than to explore on their own? Likewise, what better way to help them explore their sexual desire without putting themselves at risk for STDs, pregnancy, and all the emotional ramifications of sex with other people? I'm not the surgeon general and won't get asked to resign for saying so. But conservatives would be outraged. Why? Because they are stuck in the old, rigid ways of thinking about teenagers—particularly teenage girls—and of believing that any teenage sex is inexplicably, unfoundedly immoral. They are determined to hold on to their beloved abstinence education, which has done not one thing for the state of sexual behavior in our culture, except encourage extremely detrimental shame.

4. Talk about Emotions

In our cultural landscape, sex and sexual feelings are too often removed from emotions, and yet for most people, they are intricately entwined. When we don't talk about the ways teenagers might feel about having sex or sexual activity, we ignore an essential part of sex education, one that can make all the difference when kids decide to engage in those activities. They need to examine their expectations about sexual activity—what they hope for when they engage in this way. Such a discussion also provides space for teens to discuss how peers and their parents receive their behaviors and whether they are prepared for the repercussions of various sexual acts.

FIGHTING THE WAVES

We live in a culture in which the determinations of who a girl must be are like tidal waves crashing, one after another. Try to recover from one, thinness, and another wave, breast size, comes quickly after to knock you down once more. When parents ask me how to fight the waves, I tell them they can't. But they can do a few things to move the odds a little more in their daughters' favor.

If girls can believe that their bodies and minds exist for something other than boys' gazes and preoccupation, they might have a chance. Maybe they will become interested in sports, art, theater, history, math, writing, singing, guitar—anything, really, other than boys.

A girl's sexual self is tightly tied to a girl's body image. We know, for instance, that overweight girls are more likely to be sexually active than those who are not overweight.[6] Most marketing for teen girls focuses on what they look like and whether boys will like them. They must be thin, Caucasian or with Caucasian features, and flawless. Nothing else will do. Girls' bodies are so commoditized that it is extremely difficult for a girl to understand her body as fine just the way it is. When girls look in the mirror, it is not really to see themselves but to assess themselves, and inevitably to decide that what they see is not good enough. Girls are continual victims of themselves. For being so self-conscious, their lack of awareness about this is disturbing.

Lauren Greenfield captures this in her collection of photographs titled *Girl Culture*.[7] In most every photo a girl is on stage in some way. She is being looked at—not seen, but assessed, evaluated. Many of the photos include mirrors inside which the girls examine themselves. As Joan Jacobs Brumberg, author of *The Body Project*, says in the introduction of Greenfield's collection, "Ultimately, Greenfield's work makes the ironic point that in spite of how much American women and girls look at themselves, we are not a self-reflective society."

Part of how we help girls battle the waves and own their identities is by having them do something other than sitting in front of the mirror, by encouraging them to be subjects instead of objects. Sports are an excellent way to encourage a girl to use her body in such a way that she understands it has more purpose in the world than just to be looked at. Girls in sports often focus on making their bodies strong rather than thin, because they can see that strength has more purpose for their goals—to succeed as an athlete—than being skinny. On teams they work together, as a unified group, for a goal that doesn't involve boys. Of course, some girl-heavy sports, such as cheerleading, can be more about what a girl looks like than how she feels. There is nothing wrong, of course, with wanting to look good, and parents should not try to encourage their daughters away from an interest in their looks or clothes. The key is to support their sense of selves, whatever that may be.

Sports work well to protect a girl's body image, but really, anything that can keep a girl's attention that isn't a boy, anything that can build a sense of self-efficacy, of confidence, is prohibitive of a girl focusing every thought on boys. This might include the arts, or music, or academics. When a girl has something that makes her feel worthwhile in the world—something other than a boy's attention—she has the opportunity to defy the cultural pressure to think only about how to make herself attractive to boys.

This is what happened to me. My interest in writing grew, I got some encouragement, and I came to have a sense of myself as a writer, not just a potential girlfriend.

Of course, this is easier said than done. Remember the strength of those waves. They are powerful, withstanding. Feminism and human rights work have barely touched them. The waves have even grown bigger. They've taken on more ways—the Internet, the cell phone—to pound girls with their messages. It is so very necessary to be continually aware of that tidal-wave culture.

One of the activities I like to do with girls is to have them find at least five images in their daily lives that give them a message about their sexual identities. The girls come back to me with many more than five images. They have magazines and phrases scribbled down from bathroom stalls. They have television shows and older men checking them out from their cars. They've got billboards and bus boards and posters. One had porn magazines she found in her brother's closet. They come back angry. Some come back nonplussed, perhaps desensitized to our hypersexualized culture. Then we discuss what the messages mean and who the girls want to be in the world. They tell me their truths about the boys they like and what they've done and how it made them feel—the good stuff and the bad. And I listen, which is all they want.

If parents could do this for their girls, if they support their girls as they question the culture they live in, they will help them to be a little stronger against those waves. My hope is that with this kind of support, mothers like Jo, who we met at the beginning of this chapter, will have daughters who are much more powerful in the world than their mothers felt they were as teens.

Recently, I received an email from a woman who didn't want me to know her name. She described her years of loose-girl behavior and how no one knows. She wrote, "I've spent my whole life hiding from the world, from myself. At this point I don't know who I am or what I want. I'm lost…I wish we could talk honestly about ourselves, but loose girls can't do that. The shame is eating me alive." This brave woman's pain is not that she had sex. Her pain comes from feeling silenced, from living an unnecessarily unspeakable life.

My hope is that this book begins some movement toward cracking that silence, toward the conversations we need to have with one another, and toward the transformation we need in our culture to change the direction teen girls have been herded into for so long. We *must* have these conversations. We must speak honestly. We must be louder.

Mostly, we have to tell our stories, because in our stories lie salvation for other girls and women. It seems so cliché—stories save lives. But that's true. It was a story that laid the foundation for my own healing. I was a senior in high school, seventeen years old, and I took an elective English class called Minority Voices. We read stories about teenage girls who felt lonely, exiled, confused about who they were, and my whole world broke open: I wasn't alone. There were others out there who felt what I felt. There were others expressing what I couldn't yet express. This changed everything for me. Not yet, not in a tangible way. I was still going to hurt myself again and again. I was still going to let every crush I had, every boy who looked my way, consume my brain. I was still going to choose boys over self-enhancement. But those stories were there, in the back of my mind. They lingered. They made me want to write. And eventually, I found a way to write my own story, hoping a girl would one day read it and see herself, would keep my story in the back of her mind, and would one day tell her story, too—all these stories in a round, all these stories breaking the silence.

PART THREE

RESOURCES

APPENDIX

FOR SCHOOL ADMINISTRATORS
Discussion Questions

1. What sorts of things do you think students learn about sex at school? In particular, what do girls learn?
2. How are sex-related issues currently addressed in your school? What needs to be addressed in a more effective way, and what needs addressing at all?
3. If abstinence is in your school's sex education curriculum, is it aimed primarily at girls? What is the message connected to abstinence at your school?
4. Are cultural messages and cultural expectations exposed inside your school's sex-education curriculum?
5. Are school counselors trained in how to deal with sex and relationship issues among the students?

SUGGESTED SEX-EDUCATION EXERCISES
Girls Will Be Girls

1. Students should find examples of expectations for girls in their culture. They will likely find them in commercials, ads, magazine articles, and other media.
2. Next, students write up sentences: According to [the ad, the article], I need to be _____ to get/have _____.
3. Have students work in groups to design their own ad campaign to support girls' self-esteem. Point to some of the ad campaigns already in existence—one example is Nike, or the Dove Real Beauty Campaign.
4. Have students design hypothetical organizations that they feel girls could use, such as ones that encourage girls in sports or science.
5. Students then should start over but go through the exact same process for boys.

Ms. X

Students write questions for a teen sex-advice column. They can be real questions they have or questions they would expect to see in such a column. Put the questions into a hat and have them each choose one. Then, they work in twos to answer each question as though they were Ms. X. Finally, discuss their Ms. X answers as a class, encouraging them to pay attention to the question, What about girls' desire?

SUGGESTED TRAINING CURRICULUM FOR SCHOOL COUNSELORS DEALING WITH SEX AND RELATIONSHIP ISSUES

1. Discuss what counselors see from girls versus boys regarding sex and relationships.

2. Explore examples of what girls versus boys are taught via the prevailing culture (use magazine ads, round-ups of television shows, and so on).

3. Discuss in small groups adults' own assumptions about teenage girls' sexual desires and desires about relationships. Open this up to the larger group to share discoveries.

4. Share worksheets for dealing with loose-girl feelings and handling loose-girl behavior.

5. Hand out two or three cases of loose-girl behavior from a student and have counselors role-play how they would respond to the student and address the behavior.

FOR PARENTS AND CARETAKERS
Tips for Talking about Sex with Your Teenage Girls

1. Use simple, straightforward language. Know that your adolescent is intelligent, probably savvy, and well aware when someone is being dishonest or circumspect. Respect your teen as emotionally intelligent. Trust that she knows what she wants. You are only there to help her safely get what she wants.

2. Don't assume heterosexuality. Actually, don't assume anything about your teen when it comes to sex.

3. Avoid "the talk"—a onetime conversation—and instead continue to be available for open communication about sex with your teen. This means being open to questions, asking her questions when you feel concerned, and talking regularly about the cultural messages in media that your teen sees and absorbs each day.

4. Learn about warning signs for as many issues as you can. In particular, know how to identify depression, anxiety, sex abuse, and self-harming sexual behavior. If you see enough signs to feel concerned, step in immediately. The sooner you acknowledge issues and get help, the better chance she will have.

5. Talk about safe sex—both physically and emotionally. Educate your teen about contraception. Take her to a gynecologist. But also talk about the fact that sex can create feelings you don't expect.

6. Talk minimally about your own experiences. Always consider before sharing a story whether the story will truly help her.

In general, err on the side of silence when it comes to your own sexual experiences. It's a rare instance that your daughter needs to know anything about your past sex life.

7. Model self-care. Make yourself as conscious as you can of your sexual and relational behavior. Do your own therapy. Spend some time examining yourself. How much do you need, chase, and respond to male attention? How careful are you with your sex-related choices? What is your relationship with your partner? In other words, what are you teaching your daughter about intimacy? Do you have the sort of relationship you wish for your daughter? How do you treat the females in your world? What are you showing to your daughter about how she should feel about herself as a female—about what makes her worthwhile?

FOR COUNSELORS AND THERAPISTS AND SELF-HELP FOR POTENTIAL LOOSE GIRLS
Loose-Girl Behavior Assessment

1. Do you often use sex to get something—such as long-term love or a sense of worth—from your sex partner?
2. Do you use other aspects of male attention to gain a sense of worth or desirability?
3. Have you often avoided all else in your evening out, your work, your life, in pursuit of that attention?
4. Do you feel that you are needy?
5. Do you feel that your neediness makes you unlovable?
6. Do you hold fantasies that romantic interests will "save" you from deep-seated pain?
7. Have you more than a few times had sex with someone you didn't want to have sex with simply because he wanted to?
8. Do you need every romantic encounter you have—sexual or not—to turn into long-term love, as opposed to consciously thinking about and making choices about whether the person is someone with whom you'd actually want such a long-term relationship?
9. Do you often feel dissatisfied in your romantic relationships?
10. Have you given up adventures and self-betterment through travel, schooling, and so on, because you didn't want to be away from a romantic interest or the possibility of male attention?

If you answered yes to at least half (five) of these questions, you likely have loose-girl behavior.

CRITERIA FOR SEX AND LOVE ADDICTION

Addiction experts have identified the following criteria. If you answer yes to all or most of these, you likely have addictive romantic behavior.

1. Loss of time with family members, hobbies, and friends
2. An experience of being "high" followed by secrecy and shame
3. Negative consequences (which may include health problems and financial problems)
4. Obsessive preoccupation with the relationship or sex
5. Attempts to stop your behavior (or obsession) fail and bring considerable irritability and distress
6. Your behavior becomes riskier and more intense

The Sex and Love Addicts Anonymous website has a forty-question self-assessment to determine whether you have the signs of sex and love addiction (www.slaafws.org/download/core-files/The_40_Questions_of_SLAA.pdf).

—From Kelly McDaniel, *Ready to Heal: Women Facing Love, Sex, and Relationship Addiction* (Carefree, AZ: Gentle Path Press, 2008), 31–32.

WORKSHEETS AND EXERCISES

The following provides cognitive-behavioral approaches to build awareness about and to treat loose-girl behavior.

Build Awareness

When a boy loves me, that means I am _____.

When I don't have a boy wanting me, I believe I am _____.

When I am needy, I do _____, and believe I am

_____.

Hold on to the first list set below, and after every encounter with a boy, rewrite a new list set based on what happened. Compare the lists to see what you want versus what you actually get.

When I engage sexually with a boy, I want most

1. for example, to believe I'm desirable
2.
3.
4.
5.

When I engage sexually with a boy, I actually get

1. for example, momentary physical attention
2.
3.
4.
5.

Tracking Triggers

Use the following chart to track events that trigger loose-girl behavior:

Date	Precipitating Event	How I Felt	Description of Loose-Girl Behavior	Outcome	How I Felt

With your therapist, review what you might have done differently in each situation.

Tracking Self-Harming Thoughts

Use the following chart to track thoughts that trigger loose-girl behavior:

Date	Precipitating Event	What I Told Myself	How I Felt	Description of Loose Girl Behavior

With your therapist, determine how your false beliefs set off loose-girl behavior and how you might better deal with those damaging thoughts.

What I Told Myself	Outcome	What I Told Myself	How I Felt

RESOURCES
Sex and Relationship Websites for Teens

www.goaskalice.columbia.edu

Go Ask Alice! is the health-related Q&A Internet resource provided through Columbia University's Health Services. It aims to provide "reliable, accurate, accessible, culturally competent information and a range of thoughtful perspectives so that they can make responsible decisions concerning their health and well-being."

www.gURL.com

The site gURL.com is for teenage girls. It includes honest content about sexuality and sexual health, including advice from other teens and stores of information about various sex topics. The site has a membership option so girls can give their own advice and talk to one another on the "Shout Out" boards.

www.midwestteensexshow.com

The Midwest Teen Sex Show is a video show about teen sexuality. These guys are comedians, and they are hilarious, but they also provide accurate, thoughtful, and useful information to teenagers in an entertaining manner, all through episodes you can watch on the site.

www.plannedparenthood.org

Planned Parenthood is well known internationally as a frank, accessible provider of reproductive health care, women's health information, and sex education. A section of the Planned Parenthood website is devoted to teen sexual health and information.

www.scarleteen.com

Scarleteen: Sex Ed for the Real World is a grassroots site working to provide sexuality education and support. Heather Corinna, the proprietor, regularly provides blogs about useful examinations of recent studies, news events, and more. There is also a message board and referral service, and the site provides teen outreach and staff training through the program CONNECT.

www.sexetc.org

Sex Etc.: Sex Education by Teens for Teens has a mission to "improve teen sexual health across the country." The website is chock-full of useful information, from a glossary of sex terms to weekly live chats with experts and opportunities for teens to create their own profile and blog.

www.slaafws.org

Sex and Love Addicts Anonymous is similar to twelve-step programs such as Alcoholics Anonymous in that it is based in religion and service to God. The site lists meetings and numerous resources, including a "test" to determine whether you likely qualify as a sex and/or love addict. Sex and Love Addicts Anonymous does not provide services for minors. Some cities have meetings for adolescents, but they are not common.

www.whatcontraceptiveareyou.com.au/compare-contraception-options

Condoms are the only contraception that provides protection against both pregnancy and STDs. But this Australian website offers an interesting breakdown of the various other contraceptive devices available. The chart includes what each contraceptive is, how long it lasts, how it works, and what to consider. The site also has a survey to discover which type of contraception works best with your lifestyle.

SELECT BOOKS ABOUT SEX AND RELATIONSHIPS FOR TEENS

Michael J. Basso. *The Underground Guide to Teenage Sexuality*, 2nd ed. (Minneapolis: Fairview Press, 2003).

This is a basic but informative, fact-based question-and-answer guide for boys and girls about sexual development.

Ruth Bell. *Changing Bodies, Changing Lives: A Book for Teens on Sex and Relationships*, 3rd ed. (New York: Three Rivers Press, 1998).

From the original *Our Bodies, Ourselves*, here is comprehensive information for boys and girls about sexuality, including quotes, poems, and writings from teenagers.

Kerry Cohen. *Loose Girl: A Memoir of Promiscuity* (New York: Hyperion, 2008).

The author's memoir about her struggle with the need for male attention.

Heather Corinna. *S.E.X.: The All-You-Need-To-Know Progressive Sexuality Guide to Get through High School and College, Illustrated ed.* (New York: De Capo Press, 2007).

Corinna, owner of the website www.scarleteen.com, provides every possible aspect of sex education to her readers in a unique, upbeat, provocative style.

Kelly Huegel. *GLBTQ: The Survival Guide for Queer and Questioning Teens* (Minneapolis: Free Spirit Publishing, 2003).
This book covers everything there is to know for queer teens or teens who are questioning their sexual orientation.

SELECT BOOKS ABOUT TEENAGERS AND SEX FOR PARENTS

Ellen Bass and Kate Kaufman. *Free Your Mind: The Book for Gay, Lesbian, and Bisexual Youth and Their Allies* (New York: Harper Perennial, 1996).

This book is about sexual orientation and intended for youths, but it is also useful for adults who need to know.

Dominic Cappello and Pepper Schwartz. *Ten Talks Parents Must Have with Their Children about Sex and Character* (New York: Hyperion, 2000).

A detailed, layered book to prep parents for talking with their kids about sex. The best part of this book are the stories and correlating discussion questions included to read with your teens.

Debra Haffner. *Beyond the Big Talk: Every Parent's Guide to Raising Sexually Healthy Teens from Middle School to High School and Beyond* (New York: Newmarket Press, 2002).

Haffner provides guidelines for sexual development and health, broken down by ages.

Logan Levkoff. *Third Base Ain't What It Used to Be: What Your Kids Are Learning About Sex Today—And How to Teach Them to Become Sexually Healthy Adults* (New York: NAL Trade, 2007).

This book covers information about what teens face today when it comes to sex and sexual health.

Ronald Moglia and Jon Knowles. *All about Sex: A Family Resource on Sex and Sexuality* (New York: Three Rivers Press, 1997).

This book provides the latest information on every imaginable aspect of sexuality, including tantric sex, human reproduction, and sexual pleasure.

Lynn Ponton. *The Sex Lives of Teenagers: Revealing the Secret World of Adolescent Boys and Girls* (New York: Plume, 2001).

Ponton's book examines a number of teen cases to demonstrate the various ways teenagers experience their sexuality.

Justin Richardson and Mark Schuster. *Everything You Never Wanted Your Kids to Know about Sex (But Were Afraid They'd Ask): The Secrets to Surviving Your Child's Sexual Development from Birth to the Teens* (New York: Three Rivers Press, 2004).

This is a humorous, fun, and thorough guide to dealing with sexuality and your child, starting from toddlerhood.

Deborah M. Roffman. *Sex and Sensibility: The Thinking Parent's Guide to Talking Sense about Sex* (New York: De Capo Press, 2001).

This is a more serious research-based but still readable guide to sex and your teens.

NOTES

INTRODUCTION

1. Courtney L. Martin, *Perfect Girls, Starving Daughters: The Frightening New Normalcy of Hating Your Body* (New York: Free Press, 2007).

2. "Facts on American Teens' Sexual and Reproductive Health," Guttmacher Institute, January 2011, www.guttmacher.org/pubs/FB-ATSRH.html.

3. Ibid.

4. Joe S. McIlhaney Jr. and Freda McKissic Bush, *Hooked: New Science on How Casual Sex Is Affecting Our Children* (Chicago: Northfield Publishing, 2008).

5. For a detailed evaluation of the studies on oxytocin and attachment, see Heather Corinna's article, "Pump Up The Vole-Ume: Talking Oxytocin," Scarleteen.com, August 4, 2010, www .scarleteen.com/blog/heather_corinna/2010/08/04/pump_up_ the_voleume_talking_oxytocin.

6. Beth A. Auslander, Michelle M. Perfect, Paul A. Succop, and Susan L. Rosenthal, "Perceptions of Sexual Assertiveness among Adolescent Girls: Initiation, Refusal, and Use of Protective Behaviors," *Journal of Pediatric Adolescent Gynecology* 20, no. 3 (2007): 157–162.

7. Michelle Fine, "Sexuality, Schooling, and Adolescent Females: The Missing Discourse of Desire," *Harvard Educational Review* 58, no. 1 (1988): 29–53.

8. Joan Jacobs Brumberg, *The Body Project: An Intimate History of American Girls* (New York: Random House, 1997). See also Margaret Mead's *Coming of Age in Samoa: A Psychological Study of Primitive Youth for Western Civilization* (New York: William Morrow and Company, 1928).

9. Hugo Schwyzer, "The Paris Paradox: How Sexualization Replaces Opportunity with Obligation," *Hugo Schwyzer Blog*, www .hugoschwyzer.net, November 9, 2010, hugoschwyzer .net/2010/11/09/the-paris-paradox-how-sexualization-replaces-opportunity-with-obligation/.

10. Volunteers completed a survey that read simply, "Describe your loose girl experience." All volunteers answered my request after having read *Loose Girl* or having become aware of it and its theme.

CHAPTER 1

1. Mary Pipher, *Reviving Ophelia: Saving the Selves of Adolescent Girls* (New York: Ballantine Books, 1994), 19.

2. Ibid., 22.

3. Anne Beattie, introduction to *At Twelve: Portraits of Young Women*, by Sally Mann (New York: Aperture, 2005), 8.

4. Shumei S. Sun, Christine M. Schubert, William Cameron Chumlea, Alex F. Roche, Howard E. Kulin, Peter A. Lee, John H. Himes, and Alan S. Ryan, "National Estimates of the Timing of Sexual Maturation and Racial Differences Among US Children," *Pediatrics* 110, no. 5 (2002): 911–919. Note that the earlier onset of puberty does not include "precocious puberty," which is when puberty occurs before the age of eight.

5. Marcia E. Herman-Giddens, Eric J. Slora, Richard C. Wasserman, Carlos J. Bourdony, Manju V. Bhapkar, Gary G. Koch, and Cynthia M. Hasemeie, "Secondary Sexual Characteristics and Menses in Young Girls Seen in Office Practice: A Study from the Pediatric Research in Office Settings Network," *Pediatrics* 99, no. 4 (1997): 505–512.

6. Julian Isherwood, "Dramatic Drop in Female Puberty," *Politiken. dk*, June 18, 2010, politiken.dk/newsinenglish/ECE998340/dramatic-drop-in-female-puberty.

7. Florence Williams, "Younger Girls, Bigger Breasts: Are Chemicals to Blame?" *Slate*, July 28 2009, www.doublex.com/section/health-science/younger-girls-bigger-breasts-are-chemicals-blame.

8. William Cameron Chumlea, Christine M. Schubert, Alex F. Roche, Howard E. Kulin, Peter A. Lee, John H. Himes, and Shumei S. Sun, "Age at Menarche and Racial Comparisons in U.S. Girls," *Pediatrics* 111, no. 1 (2003): 110–113.

9. Committee on Communications, "Children, Adolescents, and Advertising," *Pediatrics* 118, no. 6 (2006): 2563–2569.

10. Naomi Wolf, *The Beauty Myth: How Images of Beauty Are Used against Women* (New York: Harper Collins, 2002).

11. Katy Gilpatric. "Violent Female Action Characters in Contemporary American Cinema," *Sex Roles* 62, nos. 11–12 (2010): 734–746.

12. Diane E. Levin and Jean Kilbourne, *So Sexy, So Soon* (New York: Ballantine Books, 2009), 9.

13. Jessica Valenti, *The Purity Myth: How America's Obsession with Virginity Is Hurting Young Women* (Berkeley: Seal Press, 2009), 13.

14. Ibid., 30.

15. Deborah L. Tolman, *Dilemmas of Desire: Teenage Girls Talk about Sexuality* (Cambridge, MA: Harvard University Press, 2002).

16. Wolf, *Beauty Myth*, 156.

17. Marta Meana, quoted in Daniel Bergner, "What Do Women Want?" *New York Times Magazine*, January 22, 2009 , www.nytimes.com/2009/01/25/magazine/25desire-t.html.

CHAPTER 2

1. Leanne K. Lamke, "The Impact of Sex-Role Orientation on Self-Esteem in Early Adolescence," *Child Development* 53, no. 6 (1982): 1530–1535.

2. Naomi Wolf, *Promiscuities: The Secret Struggle for Womanhood* (New York: Random House, 1997), 113–114.

3. Sylvia Pagan Westphal, "Partners of Underage Girls Focus Study," *Los Angeles Times*, August 13, 1999.

4. Mike Males, "Poverty, Rape, Adult/Teen Sex: Why 'Pregnancy Prevention' Programs Don't Work," *Phi Delta Kappan* 75, no. 5 (1994): 407–410.

5. Sharon G. Elstein and Noy Davis, "Sexual Relationships Between Adult Males and Young Teen Girls: Exploring the Legal and Social Responses," *American Bar Association Center on Children and the Law*, October 1997, new.abanet.org/child/PublicDocuments/statutory_rape.pdf.

6. Gerald R. Adams and Michael D. Berzonsky, *Blackwell Handbook on Adolescence* (New York: Wiley-Blackwell, 2005).

7. William Pollack, *Real Boys: Rescuing Our Sons from the Myths of Boyhood* (New York: Owl Books, 1999).

CHAPTER 3

1. Jessica Valenti, *The Purity Myth: How America's Obsession with Virginity Is Hurting Young Women* (Berkeley: Seal Press, 2009), 24. Lynn M. Phillips, referred to later in this chapter, calls this virgin icon "the pleasing woman discourse." The pleasing woman is "pleasant, feminine, and subordinate to men," and she lacks sexual desire herself. Her entire being is based on pleasing and being in service to others, especially men.

2. Hannah Brückner and Peter S. Bearman, "After the Promise: The STD Consequences of Adolescent Virginity Pledges," *Journal of Adolescent Health* 36 (2005): 271–278.

3. Emily White, *Fast Girls: Teenage Tribes and The Myth of the Slut* (New York: Scribner, 2002).

4. Ibid.

5. Kate Snow and Kelly Hagan, "Teen Girls Hazed on N.J. High School 'Slut List,'" *Good Morning America*, September 23, 2009, abcnews.go.com/GMA/teen-girls-hazed-slut-list/story?id=8649050&tqkw=&tqshow=GMA.

6. "2009 AP-MTV Digital Abuse Study," MTV's A Thin Line Project, www.athinline.org/MTV-AP_Digital_Abuse_Study_Executive_Summary.pdf.

7. Lynn M. Phillips, *Flirting with Danger: Young Women's Reflections on Sexuality and Domination* (New York: New York University Press, 2000).

8. Ariel Levy, *Female Chauvinist Pigs: Women and the Rise of Raunch Culture* (New York: Free Press, 2005).

9. Laura Sessions Stepp, *Unhooked: How Young Women Pursue Sex, Delay Love, and Lose at Both* (New York: Riverhead Books, 2007).

10. To read the full *Marie Claire* interview, see Sarah Z. Wexler, "Confessions of a Sex Addict," *Marie Claire*, April 2008, www.marieclaire.com/sex-love/relationship-issues/articles/sex-addict-confessions.

11. Find the Jezebel.com blog post I refer to at Moe Tkacik, "Is 'Sex Addict' Memoirist Kerry Cohen Even a Slut?" April 22, 2008, jezebel.com/382609/is-sex-addict-memoirist-kerry-cohen-even-actually-a-slut. The blog post is intact, but almost all the original comments were deleted. Why? Less than a month after the posting, *Jezebel* ran into problems because their readers and bloggers were often deeply cruel and nasty. You can read about that at Lauren Lipton, "Not on Our Blog You Won't," *New York Times*, May 4, 2008, www.nytimes.com/2008/05/04/fashion/04jezebel-1.html. It seemed to me that most of the blog posts and comments that were truly mean were ones about women who had achieved success—and this at a blog created for "smart" women.

12. Erica Jong, quoted in Levy, *Female Chauvinist Pigs*, 76.

13. Phillips, *Flirting with Danger*, 52.

14. Kerry Cohen, *Loose Girl: A Memoir of Promiscuity* (New York: Hyperion, 2008). For those who are interested, I wrote about the work it took to find the meaning inside this scene in the essay Kerry Cohen, "Excavating a Moment's Truth," *Brevity* .*com*, January 2010, www.creativenonfiction.org/brevity/craft/craft_cohen1_10.htm.

15. Biddy Martin, "Feminism, Criticism, and Foucault," in *Feminism and Foucault: Reflections on Resistance*, ed. Irene Diamond and Lee Quinby (Boston: Northeastern University Press, 1988), 3–19.

CHAPTER 4

1. James Jaccard, Patricia J. Dittus, and Vivian V. Gordon, "Parent-Adolescent Congruency in Reports of Adolescent Sexual Behavior and in Communications about Sexual Behavior," *Child Development* 69, no. 1 (1998): 247–261.

2. Robert W. Blum, "Mothers' Influence on Teen Sex: Connections That Promote Postponing Sexual Intercourse," *Center for Adolescent Health and Development*, University of Minnesota, 2002, www.allaboutkids.umn.edu/presskit/MonographMS.pdf.

3. Liz Brody, "The O/Seventeen Sex Survey: Mothers and Daughters Talk about Sex," *O, The Oprah Magazine*, April 14, 2009, www.oprah.com/relationships/The-Sex-Survey-Oprah-Magazine-Womens-Sex-Survey.

4. P. Averett, "Parental Communications and Young Women's Struggle for Sexual Agency," Ph.D. diss., University of Virginia Polytechnic Institute, 2004; Virginal Blacksburg and Kimberlee S. Schear, "Factors That Contribute to, and Constrain, Conversations between Adolescent Females and Their Mothers about Sexual Matters," *Forum on Public Policy: A Journal of The Oxford Roundtable*, September 22, 2006, 4751–4872.

5. Aimee Lee Ball, "Everyone's Doing *What?*" *O, The Oprah Magazine*, April 7, 2009, www.oprah.com/relationships/Teenage-Sex-Dr-Laura-Berman-on-How-to-Talk-to-Teenagers-About-Sex.

6. D. Herbenick, M. Reece, V. Schick, S. A. Sanders, B. Dodge, and J. D. Fortenberry, "Sexual Behavior in the United States: Results from a National Probability Sample of Men and Women Ages 14-94," *Journal of Sexual Medicine*, 2010, 7 (suppl. 5), 255–265.

7. A. Das, "Masturbation in the United States," *Journal of Sex and Marital Therapy* 33, no. 4 (2007): 301–317.

8. Christine O'Donnell's now-famous television interview is available at "Christine O'Donnell's 90s Anti-Masturbation Campaign," www.msnbc.com, September 14, 2010, www.youtube.com/watch?v=RzHcqcXo_NA.

9. D. Rosenthal, S. Moore, and I. Flynn, "Adolescent Self-Efficacy, Self-Esteem, and Sexual Risk-Taking," *Journal of Community and Applied Social Psychology* 1, no. 2 (June 1991): 77–88.

10. Judith Levine, *Harmful to Minors: The Perils of Protecting Children from Sex* (New York: Thunder's Mouth Press, 2003), 160–161.

11. Lynn Ponton, *The Sex Lives of Teenagers: Revealing the Secret World of Adolescent Boys and Girls* (New York: Penguin Group, 2000).

12. Michael Reece, D. Herbenick, V. Schick, A. Sanders, B. Dodge, and J. D. Fortenberry, "Condom Use Rates in a National Probability Sample of Males and Females Ages 14 to 94 in the United States," *Journal of Sexual Medicine* 7, suppl. 5 (2010): 266–276. Interestingly, black and Hispanic adolescents use condoms the most.

13. "Patterns of Condom Use Among Adolescents: The Impact of Mother-Adolescent Communication," *American Journal of Public Health*, October 1, 1998, www.cdc.gov/std/general/ Condom_Use_Among_Adolescents.htm, www.cdc.gov, June 8, 2009, retrieved April 2, 2011.

14. Peter R. Kilmann, Jennifer M. C. Vendemia, Michele M. Parnell, and Geoffrey C. Urbaniak, "Parent Characteristics Linked with Daughters' Attachment Styles," *Adolescence* 44, no. 175 (Autumn 2009): 557–568.

15. Episode 3.10, "The Giving Tree." For the full transcript and a comparison with a sex talk that went nowhere on *My So-Called Life*, see S. Seltzer, "*On Friday Night Lights*, the TV Sex Talk Done Right," *RH Reality Check*, March 27, 2009, www.rhrealitycheck.org/blog/2009/03/26/on-friday-night-lights-tv-sex-talk-done-right. Another excellent television sex talk was between father and son on *Glee*. For the video clip, see "Watch Kurt and His Dad Have a Gay Sex Talk on *Glee*," retrieved April 2, 2011, vodpod.com/watch/5729957-watch-kurt-and-his-dad-have-a-gay-sex-talk-on-glee.

CHAPTER 5

1. Travis Plum Lee, Family Ark Ministries, March 30, 2010, retrieved January 12, 2011, www.travisplumlee.com/news/?p=131.

2. Andrew Chomik, "Her Daddy Issues," Askmen.com, retrieved April 2, 2011, www.askmen.com/dating/curtsmith_300/366_her-daddy-issues.html.

3. Trayce Hansen, "Love Isn't Enough: 5 Reasons Why Same-Sex Marriage Will Harm Children," Drtraycehansen.com, retrieved April 2, 2011, www.drtraycehansen.com/Pages/writings_samesex.html.

4. Gabriella Kortsch, "Fatherless Women: What Happens to the Adult Woman Who Was Raised without Her Father?" Trans4Mind, retrieved April 2, 2011, www.trans4mind.com/counterpoint/kortsch4.shtml.

5. Megan Fox also said, "We seek male attention to validate us and so no one can really be your friend because if she takes attention from you then your daddy doesn't love you, ultimately." See the full story at "Megan Fox: Girls Are Awful," Showbiz Spy, September 17, 2009, www.showbizspy.com/article/191974/megan-fox-girls-are-awful.html.

6. F. B. Krohn and Z. Bagan, "The Effects Absent Fathers Have on Female Development and College Attendance," *College Student Journal of Family* 35, no. 4 (2001): 598–608.

7. J. Deardorff, J. P. Ekwaru, L. H. Kushi, B. J. Ellis, L. C. Greenspan, A. Mirabedi, E. G. Landaverdi, and R. A. Hiatt, "Father Absence, Body Mass Index, and Pubertal Timing in Girls: Differential Effects by Family Income and Ethnicity," *Journal of Adolescent Health*, published online September 20, 2010, jahonline.org/article/S1054-139X(10)00389-7/abstract.

8. B. Bower, "Absent Dads Linked to Early Sex by Daughters," *Science News*, 164 (July 19, 2003): 35–36.

9. S. R. Jaffee, T. E. Moffitt, A. Caspi, and A. Taylor, "Life with (or without) Father: The Benefits of Living with Two Biological Parents Depend on the Father's Antisocial Behavior," *Child Development* 74, no. 1 (2003): 109–126.

10. The quotes I use can be found in the scenes captured here: Tracey Egan Morrissey, "Purity Balls: Protecting Girls from Making Choices," *Jezebel.com*, January 4, 2010, jezebel.com/5440014/purity-balls-protecting-girls-from-making-choices.

CHAPTER 6

1. J. I. Dolgan, "Depression in Children," *Pediatric Annals* 19, no. 1 (1990): 45–50.

2. Thomas J. Dishion, "Cross-Setting Consistency in Early Adolescent Psychopathology: Deviant Friendships and Problem Behavior Sequelae," *Journal of Personality* 68, no. 6 (2000): 1109–1126.

3. Anthony Biglan, C. W. Metzler, R. Wirt, D. Ary, J. Noell, L. Ochs, C. French, and D. Hood, "Social and Behavioral Factors Associated with High-Risk Sexual Behavior among Adolescents," *Journal of Behavioral Medicine* 13, no. 3 (1990): 245–261.

4. "Study Links Teen Drug and Alcohol Use with Promiscuity," CNN.com, December 7, 1999, articles.cnn.com/1999-12-07/us/teens.drugs.sex_1_teens-alcohol-drugs?_s=PM:US.

5. P. A. Cavazos-Rehg, E. L. Spitznagel, K. K. Bucholz, K. Norberg, W. Reich, I. Nurnberger Jr, V. Hesselbrock, J. Kramer, S. Kuperman, L. J. Bierut, "The Relationship between Alcohol Problems and Dependence, Conduct Problems and Diagnosis, and Number of Sex Partners in a Sample of Young Adults," *Alcoholism: Clinical and Experimental Research* 31, no. 12 (2007): 2046–2052.

6. Sophie Borland, "Legacy of the Ladette: Now Alarming Rise in Teenage Promiscuity and Abortions Is Linked to Women's Binge Drinking," *Mail Online*, August 21, 2010, www .dailymail.co.uk/news/article-1304833/The-Legacy-ladette-binge-drinking-women-linked-rise-casual-sex-abortions-prescriptions-morning-pill.html#ixzz18ItsxRCX.

7. Sheila B. Blume, "Sexuality and Stigma: The Alcoholic Woman," *Alcohol Health and Research World* 15, no. 2 (1991): 139–46. For a recent discussion of examples of blaming the victim regarding rape, see Elaine Grant, "A New Era in Handling Campus Rape," New Hampshire Public Radio, April 4, 2011, retrieved April 5, 2011, www.nhpr.org/new-era-handling-campus-rape.

8. It remains intensely difficult to untangle what really is standard or normal when the culture has determined for us already that no sex in any way is normal for a teen. Suddenly, the question of whether a behavior causes someone extreme distress—a typical psychologist's question when determining whether behavior needs to be addressed—becomes doubtful: a girl may well feel tremendous shame about behavior that isn't so horrible when that behavior is removed from cultural mores. We have to wonder whether the real trouble is the behavior or the labeling of the behavior as a problem.

9. Craig Nakken, *The Addictive Personality*, 2nd ed. (Center City, MN: Hazelden Publishing, 1988).

10. Kelly McDaniel, *Ready to Heal: Women Facing Love, Sex, and Relationship Addiction* (Carefree, AZ: Gentle Path Press, 2008), 9. For the leading experts' words on love and sex addiction, see also Pia Mellody's *Facing Love Addiction: Giving Yourself the Power to Change the Way You Love* (New York: HarperCollins, 1992) and Patrick Carnes's *Out of the Shadows: Understanding Sex Addiction* (Center City, MN: Hazelden Publishing, 2001).

11. E. O. Paolucci, M. L. Genuis, and C. Violato, "A Meta-Analysis of the Published Research on the Effects of Child Sexual Abuse," *Journal of Psychology* 135, no. 1 (2001): 17–36.

12. Heather Corinna, "Who's Calling Who Compulsive? Calling Out a Common Rape Survivor Stereotype," Scarleteen.com, June 6, 2010, www.scarleteen.com/blog/heather_corinna/2010/06/06/whos_calling_who_compulsive_calling_out_a_common_rape_survivor_stere.

13. Becky and Kathy Liddle, "More Than Good Intentions: How to Be an Ally to the Gay, Lesbian, Bisexual, and Transgender Community," *Auburn Gay/Lesbian/Bisexual Caucus*, retrieved April 5, 2011, www.auburn.edu/aglbc/ally.htm.

CHAPTER 7

1. "Facts on American Teens' Sexual and Reproductive Health," Guttmacher Institute, January 2011, www.guttmacher.org/pubs/FB-ATSRH.html.

2. Laura M. Carpenter, *Virginity Lost: An Intimate Portrait of First Sexual Experiences* (New York: New York University Press, 2005).

3. The Henry J. Kaiser Family Foundation and *Seventeen* Magazine, "Virginity and the First Time: A Series of National Surveys of Teens about Sex," Henry J. Kaiser Family Foundation, October 2003, www.kff.org/entpartnerships/upload/Virginity-and-the-First-Time-Summary-of-Findings.pdf.

4. Bill Albert, "National Campaign to Prevent Teen Pregnancy, 'With One Voice 2007: America's Adults and Teens Sound Off about Teen Pregnancy: A Periodic National Survey,'" The National Campaign to Prevent Teen and Unplanned Pregnancy, February 2007, www.thenationalcampaign.org/resources/pdf/pubs/WOV2007_fulltext.pdf.

5. Judith Levine, *Harmful to Minors: The Perils of Protecting Children from Sex* (New York: Thunder's Mouth Press, 2003), 160.

6. Kaiser Family Foundation, T. Hoff, L. Greene, and J. Davis, "National Survey of Adolescence and Young Adults: Sexual Health Knowledge, Attitudes and Behaviors," Henry J. Kaiser Family Foundation, May 2003, www.kff.org/youthhivstds/upload/National-Survey-of-Adolescents-and-Young-Adults-Sexual-Health-Knowledge-Attitudes-and-Experiences-Summary-of-Findings.pdf.

7. S. A. Vannier and L. F. O'Sullivan, "Sex without Desire: Characteristics of Occasions of Sexual Compliance in Young Adults' Committed Relationships," *Journal of Sex Research* 47, no. 5 (2010): 429–439.

8. Latoya Peterson, "The Not-Rape Epidemic," in *Yes Means Yes! Visions of Female Sexual Power and a World without Rape*, ed. Jaclyn Friedman and Jessica Valenti (Berkeley, CA: Seal Press, 2008), 209–219.

9. Lee Jacob Riggs, "A Love Letter from an Anti-Rape Activist to Her Feminist Sex-Toy Store," in Friedman and Valenti, *Yes Means Yes!*, 114.

10. Levine, *Harmful to Minors*, 89.

11. Jill Filipovic, "Offensive Feminism: The Conservative Gender Norms That Perpetuate Rape Culture, and How Feminists Can Fight Back," in Friedman and Levine, *Yes Means Yes!*, 19.

12. Sexual Abuse Statistics, Teen Help.com, retrieved April 5, 2011, www.teenhelp.com/teen-abuse/sexual-abuse-stats.html.

13. T. Luster and S. A. Small, "Sexual Abuse History and Number of Sex Partners among Female Adolescents," *Family Planning Perspectives* 29, no. 5 (1997): 204–211.

14. J. H. Beitchman, K. Zucker, J. Hood, G. DaCosta, and D. Akman, "A Review of the Long-Term Effects of Child Sexual Abuse," *Child Abuse and Neglect* 16 (1992): 101–118.

CHAPTER 8

1. National Campaign to Prevent Teen and Unplanned Pregnancy and Cosmogirl.com, "Sex and Tech, Results from a Survey of Teens and Young Adults," National Campaign to Prevent Teen and Unplanned Pregnancy, retrieved April 5, 2011, www.thenationalcampaign.org/sextech/PDF/SexTech_Summary.pdf.

2. "Home Computer Access and Internet Use," *Child Trends Databank*, June 2010, www.childtrendsdatabank.org/?q=node/298.

3. For a list of sexting legislation for each state, see "2010 Legislation Related to 'Sexting,'" National Conference of State Legislature, January 4, 2011, www.ncsl.org/default.aspx?tabid=19696.

4. For more on Jesse Logan and the *Today* show interview with Parry Aftab, see Mike Celizic, "Her Teen Committed Suicide Over 'Sexting,'" Today Parenting, March 6, 2009, today.msnbc.msn.com/id/29546030.

5. For more on Hope Witsell's story, see Michael Inbar, "'Sexting' Bullying Cited in Teen's Suicide," *Today People*, December 2, 2009, today.msnbc.msn.com/id/34236377/ns/today-today_people/.

6. Mike Brunker, "'Sexting' Surprise: Six Teens Face Child Porn Charges," MSNBC.com, January 15, 2009, www.msnbc.msn.com/id/28679588/.

7. Vicki Mabrey and David Perozzi, "'Sexting': Should Child Pornography Laws Apply?" ABCnews.com, April 1, 2010, abcnews.go.com/Nightline/phillip-alpert-sexting-teen-child-porn/story?id=10252790.

8. Berkman Center for Internet and Society, "Enhancing Child Safety & Online Technologies," Harvard University, December 31, 2008, cyber.law.harvard.edu/sites/cyber.law.harvard.edu/files/ISTTF_Final_Report-Executive_Summary.pdf.

9. Riva Richmond, "Sexting May Place Teens at Legal Risk," *New York Times*, March 26, 2009, gadgetwise.blogs.nytimes.com/2009/03/26/sexting-may-place-teens-at-legal-risk/.

10. Dawn Turner Trice, "Girls, Don't Dumb Yourselves Down in Social Media," *Chicago Tribune*, November 12, 2010, c.

11. Judith Levine, *Harmful to Minors: The Perils of Protecting Children from Sex* (New York: Thunder's Mouth Press, 2003), 149.

12. Facebook Horror Stories, True Facebook Stories, retrieved April 5, 2011, www.facebook-horror-stories.com/.

13. Russell Goldman, "Facebook Status 'Engaged,' but Cops Call It Statutory Rape," ABCnews.com, September 14, 2010, abcnews.go.com/Technology/facebook-status-read-engaged-cops-call-statutory-rape/story?id=11626836&tqkw=&tqshow=.

14. Tamar Lewin, "Teenagers' Internet Socializing Not a Bad Thing," *New York Times*, November 19, 2008, www.nytimes.com/2008/11/20/us/20internet.html?_r=1.

15. P. M. Valkenburg and J. Peter, "Social Consequences of the Internet for Adolescents: A Decade of Research," *Current Directions in Psychological Science* 18, no. 1 (2009): 1–5.

CHAPTER 9

1. Ellen Fein and Sherrie Schneider, *The Rules* (New York: Grand Central Publishing, 1995).

2. "Infidelity Statistics," Menstuff, retrieved April 5, 2011, www .menstuff.org/issues/byissue/infidelitystats.html.

CHAPTER 10

1. James O. Prochaska, John C. Norcross, and Carlo C. DiClemente, *Changing for Good: A Revolutionary Six-Stage Program for Overcoming Bad Habits and Moving Your Life Positively Forward* (New York: Avon Books, 1994).

2. Most chapters of Sex and Love Addicts Anonymous won't accommodate teenagers, which I find disturbing. Although they are difficult to find, there are a few teen programs scattered throughout the nation, such as in New York and Portland, Oregon.

CHAPTER 11

1. M. M. Bersamin, S. Walker, E. D. Waiters, D. A. Fisher, and J. W. Grube, "Promising to Wait: Virginity Pledges and Adolescent Sexual Behavior," *Journal of Adolescent Health* 36, no. 5 (2005): 428–436.

2. Jocelyn M. Elders, foreword to Levine, *Harmful to Minors*, ix.

3. Patricia Donovan, "Falling Teen Pregnancy, Birthrates: What's Behind the Declines?" *The Guttmacher Report on Public Policy*, vol. 1, October 1998; Steven Reinberg, "U.S. Teen Birth Rate Hit Record Low in 2009: CDC," December 21, 2009, health .msn.com/health-topics/sexual-health/birth-control/article page.aspx?cp-documentid=100268351.

4. Levine, *Harmful to Minors*, 94.

5. "Not Just Another Thing to Do: Teens Talk about Sex, Regret, and the Influence of Their Parents," The National Campaign to Prevent Teen and Unplanned Pregnancy, June 30, 2000, www .thenationalcampaign.org/resources/pdf/pubs/NotJust_FINAL.pdf.

6. A. Y. Akers, C. P. Lynch, M. A. Gold, J. C. Chang, W. Doswell, H. C. Wiesenfeld, W. Feng, and J. Bost, "Exploring the Relationship among Weight, Race, and Sexual Behaviors among Girls," *Pediatrics* 124 (2009): 913–920.

7. Joan Jacobs Brumberg, Introduction, Lauren Greenfield, *Girl Culture* (San Francisco: Chronicle Books, 2002).

ABOUT THE AUTHOR

KERRY COHEN is the author of *Loose Girl: A Memoir of Promiscuity*; the forthcoming memoir *Seeing Ezra*, about parenting her autistic son; as well as three young-adult novels, *Easy*, *The Good Girl*, and *It's Not You, It's Me*. Her work has been featured in the *New York Times* and the *Washington Post*, as well as in numerous anthologies and journals. She has appeared on *Dr. Phil*, *Saturday Live* on the BBC, and morning news shows to speak about the loose-girl issue, and she was featured on the WE Network's documentary series *The Secret Lives of Women*, about sex addiction. She is a practicing psychotherapist and writing teacher, and she lives with her family in Portland, Oregon. For more details, visit www.kerry-cohen.com.